The North Eastern Boundary Controversy
And The Aroostook War

John Francis Sprague

The North Eastern Boundary Controversy and the Aroostook War

BY JOHN FRANCIS SPRAGUE

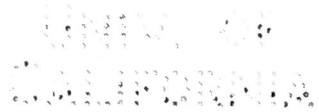

Dover, Maine
The Observer Press

The foot-note pp. 12-13 refers to the report of the commissioners made October 25, 1798.

Printing Statement:

Due to the very old age and scarcity of this book,
many of the pages may be hard to read due to the
blurring of the original text, possible missing pages,
missing text, dark backgrounds and other issues
beyond our control.

Because this is such an important and rare work, we
believe it is best to reproduce this book regardless of
its original condition.

Thank you for your understanding.

JOHN FAIRFIELD
GOVERNOR OF MAINE, 1839

The North Eastern Boundary Controversy and the Aroostook War

By John Francis Sprague

A SERIOUS disagreement existed between the United States and Great Britain from the treaty of peace (1783) to the Webster–Ashburton treaty (1842), respecting the boundary line between what is now and was in 1842, the State of Maine and Canada, and known in history as the Northeast Frontier.

In tracing back to the sources of this contention, which was acute for more than a half century, it seems to me that two causes were among the earliest and most predominating which led up to the general confusion.

The first was the fact that the English sovereigns were very ignorant of American geography and were perpetually making grants of lands irreconcilably and often grotesquely conflicting, and the second was the instinctive desire of the Anglo Saxon to possess himself of all of the territory of this earth within his reach.

In 1493, Alexander VI, Pope of Rome, issued a bull, granting the New World, which Columbus had discovered, to the sovereigns of Spain and Portugal.

In that age a papal bull was generally regarded by Christian nations as a sufficient title to heathen lands, and under this title Spain claimed the entire North American coast from Cape Florida to Cape Breton.

France, although a Catholic nation, was in unison with England, which had then become Protestant, in protesting against such an exclusive and unfair grant.

So far as there was an issue between England and Spain about American territory it was settled by Sir Francis Drake in 1588, by the victory over the Spanish Armada in the British Channel, which has been the scene of so many famous naval battles and where so much of the world's history has been made.

But England had not submitted to the slow process of waiting for the God of battles to determine her rights by discovery and conquest as they then stood in the western hemisphere. In 1495-6, three years after its discovery and before Columbus had seen it, Henry VII, King of England, issued a commission to John Cabot and his sons, "to seek out, discover and find whatsoever Isles, Countries, Regions or Provinces of the heathens and infidels" hitherto unknown to all Christians, and, as vassals of the king, to hold the same by his authority.

In 1502, the same king issued authority to Hugh Eliot and Thomas Ashurst to discover and take possession of the "Islands and Continents" in America.

As early as 1524 and many years before England had actually asserted jurisdictional rights on this continent, Francis I, King of France, doubted the "clause in Adam's will" which made this continent the incontrovertible possession of "his brothers of Spain and Portugal" and sent out discoverers and explorers, who explored the entire coast from the thirtieth to the fiftieth degree of latitude, and named the whole region New France.

Ten years later Jacques Quartier, known in English history as "Cartier," commissioned by the same king, made several voyages to America and took possession of Canada. The French government maintained it ever after until its titles were lost by treaties and conquest.

On the 8th of November, 1603, Henry IV, King of France, appointed Pier de Monts, his lieutenant-general, in the country, territories, coast and limits of Cadia, (la Cadia) since called Acadia, commencing at the fortieth degree and thence to the forty-sixth degree.

By charter of the 10th of September, 1621, James I granted to Sir William Alexander, a certain territory, under the name of "Nova Scotia," with the following boundaries: "Beginning at Cape Sable, in forty-three degrees north latitude, or thereabout, extending thence westwardly along the seashore, to the road commonly called St. Mary's Bay; thence towards the north by a direct line crossing the entrance or mouth of that great ship road, which runs into the eastern tract of land between the territories of the Souriquois and of the Etchemins, (Bay of Fundy) to the river commonly called St. Croix, and to the most remote spring or source, which, from the western part thereof, first mingles itself with the river aforesaid; from thence, by an imaginary direct line, which may be conceived to stretch through the land, or to run towards the north, to the nearest road, river or spring emptying itself into the great river de Canada (River St. Lawrence); and from thence proceeding eastwardly along the seashores of the said river de Canada, to the river, road, port, or shore, commonly known and called by the name of Gachepe or Gaspe; and thence south-eastwardly to the islands called Baccaleos or Cape Breton, leaving these islands on the right and the gulf of the said river de Canada or of the great ship road and the lands of Newfoundland, with the islands to the same pertaining, on the left; and thence to the head land or promontory of Cape Breton aforesaid, lying near the latitude of forty-five degrees, or thereabout; and from the said promontory of Cape Breton, towards the south and west, to Cape Sable afore-

said, where the perambulation began, * * * * *
all which lands aforesaid, shall at all times hereafter be
called and known by the name of Nova Scotia, or New
Scotland, in America.''

Albert Gallatin in his introduction to ''The Right of
the United States of America to the North Eastern
Boundary Claimed by Them,'' (1840) says:

''The western boundary thereby assigned to Nova
Scotia differs from the eastern boundary of the United
States, as described by the treaty of peace of 1783, in
the following particulars.

''1st. The western source of the river St. Croix was
intended by Sir William Alexander's charter; but by
the treaty of 1783, the said river from its mouth to its
source, without particularly designating which source, is
made the boundary; and this has been decided to be the
river from its mouth to the source of its north branch.

''2nd. The line from the source of the River St.
Croix, is, according to the charter, to run towards the
north; (versus septentrionem;) by the treaty, it must
run due north, or directly north.

''3rd. The said line, by the charter, extends to the
river St. Lawrence, and, by the treaty, to the highlands
dividing the rivers, &c.''

On the 3d of April, 1639, Charles I granted to
Ferdinand Gorges, by the name of Province or Country
of Maine, a territory bounded on the west by Piscataway Harbor and the river Newichewanocke, (Piscataqua
River) to the farthest head thereof, and thence one hundred and twenty miles northwestwards, extending from
Piscataway Harbor, northeastwards, along the seacoast
to Sagadahock, (the river Kennebec below the confluence
of the river Androscoggin,) and up the river thereof to
Kynybecky River, and, through the same, to the head
thereof, and into the land northwestwards one hundred

and twenty miles from the mouth of Sagadahock, Etc.

This last named grant was purchased in the year 1674, by the Colony of Massachusetts.

By the twelfth article of the treaty of Utrecht, in 1713, "the Most Christian King of France" ceded to the Queen of England in perpetuity Acadia or Nova Scotia entire, "according to its ancient boundaries," Etc.

But what its "ancient boundaries" were was for nearly fifty years after the treaty of Utrecht a matter of dispute between England and France and more especially between the pioneers and settlers of New France, and the Massachusetts Colony and the inhabitants of the Province of Maine, who had settled east of the Kennebec River.

The Governor of New France contended that the ancient bounds of Acadia extended as far west as the Kennebec River under the grant of Charles I to Gorges, and had never been changed by any act of England.

Attempts at a settlement were made between the two governments at various times but the results were futile.

When Wolfe conquered Quebec in 1759, all of Canada passed to the domain of the English by conquest and the minor questions of boundary lines were lost sight of.

Incidental to this long contention as to what was the westerly line of Acadia, was the destruction of the Jesuit Mission at Norridgewock and the killing of its missionary, Father Sebastian Ralé, in 1724, by the Massachusetts colonists.

Gallatin in the work above referred to, in speaking of this Gorges grant and its subsequent purchase by the Colony of Massachusetts, asserts that it throws no light on the question as to how England acquired any title to the territory between the Kennebec and St. Croix, and says: "Although the name of Maine has since been extended to the country, eastwardly, as far as the boundaries of Nova Scotia, the ancient Province of Maine, according to the aforesaid original grant, was bounded on the east by the river Sadahock or Kennebec.''

These facts are only referred to here, parenthetically, for the purpose of calling attention to the generally chaotic condition of the sources of the jurisdictional rights of England in the Province of Maine, at the time of the treaty of peace in 1783.

The English had themselves, whether wrongfully or rightfully, whether by overt acts or not, made permanent the title of Massachusetts to the Province of Maine as far east as the St. Croix River, but how far north it extended was another matter and one of the principal causes of all the trouble between the people of Maine and New Brunswick and the American and English governments.

In the several treaties between France and England ceding to each other Acadia, no specific mention is made of boundaries, so the student is obliged to rely upon the grants from the English crown to its subjects for information as to what was the original intent of the English government, regarding the northerly line of the Province of Maine.

On the 12th day of March, 1663, Charles II granted to his brother James, Duke of York, "all that part of the main land of New England, beginning at a certain place, called or known by the name of St. Croix adjoining to New Scotland in America, and from thence extending along the sea coast, into a place called Pemaquin or Pemaquid, and so up the river thereof to the furtherest head of the same as it tendeth northward to the river of Kennebec and so up, by the shortest course, to the river of Canada, northwards.''

All authorities agreed that the name "Maine" at some time in some way extended over all the above described territory and that the river Kennebec was what was in the ancient maps Sadahock, and that "the river Canada" was the river St. Lawrence.

October 7th, 1691, William and Mary, by grant, annexed to the charter of the Massachusetts Colony, Nova Scotia, the ancient Province of Maine, and Sagadahock, or the Duke of York's grant, containing however, this proviso, "and it is our royal will and pleasure that no grants of any lands lying or extending from the river Sagadahock (Kennebec) to the Gulf of St. Lawrence and Canada rivers, (St. Lawrence River) and to the main sea northward and eastward, to be made or passed by the Governor and General Assembly of our said Province, be of any force, validity, or effect, until we, our assigns and successors shall have signified our or their approbation of the same."

This grant is valuable herein, only for the purpose of showing that the English then claimed territory as far north as the St. Lawrence.

There does not seem to be any reason for this grant of Nova Scotia or Acadia to Massachusetts, which had been restored to France by the treaty of Breda, other than the fact that a state of war existed between the nations in 1691.

By the treaty of Ryswick, (1697) Great Britain, however, agreed to restore to France "all countries, islands, forts and colonies, wheresoever situated, which the French did possess before the declaration of war."

The Massachusetts Colony asserted jurisdiction over all of that part of the Province of Maine annexed to their charter by William and Mary, which was situated east of the Kennebec River, and the last claim of the French to this territory was extinguished with the destruction of the Kennebec Mission in 1724.

Subsequent to this a question arose among the colonists as to their legal title to the territory between the Kennebec and St. Croix, which was referred to the attorney and solicitor general of the crown, who gave it as their opinion (Aug. 11, 1731) "that all the tract of land lying between the rivers of Kennebec and St. Croix, is granted by their charter to the inhabitants of the said Province; that the rights of government granted to the said Province extend over this tract of land."

In Mitchell's map in the year 1755, the river St. Croix, in accordance with their decision, and a due north line from its source to the river St. Lawrence, are made the boundary between Nova Scotia and New England.

And Gallatin says that "in this map the river St. Croix, and a due north line from its source to the river St. Lawrence, are, accordingly, made the boundary between Nova Scotia and New England; embracing, under this last designation, the eastern part of Massachusetts, by the name of Sagadahock."

Both Nova Scotia and New England are, in that map, published with the approbation of the board of trade, bounded to the north by the river St. Lawrence. And that river continued, accordingly, to be the northern boundary of both, till the 7th of October, 1763; when Canada, and all the possessions claimed by France in that quarter, having, by virtue of the treaty of peace of February, 1763, been definitively ceded by her to Great Britain, His Britannic Majesty issued a proclamation establishing new governments, and, amongst others, that of Quebec.

The boundaries of that government were, by the said proclamation, fixed as follows: "Bounded on the Labrador Coast by the river St. John; and from thence, by a line drawn from the head of that river, through the Lake St. John, to the south end of the Lake Nipissing, from whence the said line, crossing the river St. Lawrence and the Lake Champlain, in forty-five degrees of north latitude, passes along the Highlands which divide the rivers that empty themselves into the said river St. Lawrence from those which fall into the sea, and also along the north coast of the Bay des Chaleurs and the Coast of the Gulf of St. Lawrence, to Cape Rosiers; and from thence, crossing the mouth of the river St. Lawrence, by the west end of the island of Anticosti, terminates at the aforesaid river St. John.''

The Highlands designated above were thus assigned as the southern boundary of the province of Quebec and became the northern boundary of Nova Scotia; the northwest corner of which, instead of being, as heretofore, on the banks of the St. Lawrence, was thereby placed on the Highlands.

This boundary of the Province of Quebec was again ratified by the British government by the act of Parliament of the 14th, Geo. III, Chap. 83, (1774) commonly called the Quebec Act.

The treaty of peace between the Colonies and England at the close of the war of the Revolution and known in history as the treaty of 1783, provides—''And that all disputes, which might arise in the future on the subject of the boundaries of the said United States, may be prevented, it is hereby agreed and declared, that teh following are and shall be their boundaries, viz: From the northwest angle of Nova Scotia, viz: that angle which is formed by a line drawn due north from the source of the St. Croix River, to the Highlands, which divide those rivers, that empty themselves into the river St. Lawrence from those which fall into the Atlantic Ocean, to the northwesternmost head of Connecticut River; east, by a line to be drawn along the middle of the river St. Croix, from its mouth in the Bay of Fundy to its source; and from its source, directly north, to the aforesaid Highlands, which divide the rivers which fall into the Atlantic Ocean from those that fall into the river St. Lawrence.''

Subsequent to this treaty doubts arose as to which was the St. Croix River, and commissioners were appointed under the provisions of its fifth article who declared October 25, 1798, that a river called "Scoodiac," and the northern branch of it (called "Cheputnaticook") to be the true river St. Croix as intended by the treaty, that its mouth was in the Bay of Passamaquoddy at a place called Joe's Point, and its source at the northern-most head spring of the northern branch aforesaid.

Jay's Treaty

During the War of 1812 the British seized and held Moose Island on which the city of Eastport now stands, and at the treaty of Ghent they refused to restore it.

It was generally stipulated that all territory, places, and possessions taken by either party during the war should be restored, and it was specially provided that such of the islands in Passamaquoddy Bay as were claimed by both parties, should remain in the possession of the party in whose occupation they might be at the time of the exchange or the ratification of the treaty, without prejudice to either party, till the question of title should be settled.   For such a settlement Art. IV provided that the question should be referred to two commissioners to be appointed by the two governments.

The King of Great Britain appointed Thomas Barclay and President Madison appointed John Holmes, who was a resident of the Province or District of Maine.

Their decision, which was rendered November 24, 1817, seems to have been acquiesced in by all parties and with a few exceptions I do not find that it was very seriously criticised by the writers at that time.*

*The first question that arose before these commissioners was, which of the three rivers falling into the Bay of Fundy was the St. Croix contemplated by the treaty of 1783.

It was well understood by both governments that the boundary line of Nova Scotia was left very indefinite by the treaty of 1783, but as there were but few settlers on the disputed territory and but little business or commerce, and as both nations were engrossed in struggles with each other of more consequence, there was but little controversy about it.

The fact was, however, recognized by the treaty of Ghent (1814) and they made provision for its adjustment

These rivers had all been known and described at various times by the name of St. Croix. The most easterly had likewise been called the Magaquadavic; the intermediate, the Schoodic; the most westerly, the Cobscook.

The decision of the commissioners was that the middle river, known sometimes as the Schoodic, was the true St. Croix River. It having been thus fixed, it was so regarded by both governments, at the treaty of Ghent, and in the proceedings when the whole matter was finally adjusted by the Webster-Ashburton treaty.

It has, however, been the opinion of students of history who have since investigated the subject, that a grave error was committed, by which the American government, and ultimately the State of Maine, were grossly wronged, that if the subject had been properly considered and fairly adjudicated, the easterly river, rather than the Schoodic or the intermediate river, would have been the easterly boundary of the State of Maine.

Probably no man in the days of this controversy gave the subject more consideration than the late Col. John G. Deane of Portland, and formerly of Ellsworth. He was a leading member of the Legislature during that time and was the author of several official reports relating to the North Eastern Boundary, and he was firmly convinced that the commissioners selected the wrong river for the St. Croix.

By this blunder, if such it were, Col. Deane estimated that the State of Maine "lost a strip of territory from fifteen to twenty miles in breadth, and one hundred and seventy-five miles in length."

(See a sketch of the life of John G. Deane, Maine Hist. Coll. 2d Series, Vol. 1, p. 179. "The North Eastern Boundary," by Israel Washburn, Jr., read before the Maine Historical Society, May 15, 1879.)

by the fifth article of this treaty, a part of which is as
follows:

"Whereas neither that point of the Highlands lying
due north from the source of the River St. Croix, and
designated in the former treaty of Peace between the
two Powers, as the north-west angle of Nova Scotia, nor
the north-western most head of the Connecticut River,
has yet been ascertained; and whereas that part of the
boundary line between the Dominions of the two Powers,
which extends from the source of the River St. Croix,
directly north, to the above-mentioned north-west angle
of Nova Scotia; thence, along the said Highlands which
divide those rivers that empty themselves into the River
St. Lawrence from those which fall into the Atlantic
Ocean, to the north-western most head of Connecticut
River; thence, down along the middle of that river, to
the forty-fifth degree of north latitude; thence, by a line
due west, on said latitude, until it strikes the River
Iroquois or Cataraquy, has not yet been surveyed; it is
agreed that for those several purposes, two Commissioners
shall be appointed, sworn and authorized to act, &c.
* * * * * * * The said Commissioners shall
have power to ascertain and determine the points above
mentioned, in conformity with the provisions of the said
treaty of Peace of 1783, and shall cause the boundary
aforesaid, from the source of the River St. Croix to the
River Iroquois or Cataraquy, to be surveyed and marked
according to the said provisions. The said Commissioners shall make a map of the said boundary and annex to
it a declaration under their hands and seals, certifying it
to be the true map of the said boundary, and particular-
izing the latitude and longitude of the north-west angle
of Nova Scotia, of the north-western most head of Connecticut River, and of such other points of the said
boundary as they may deem proper. And both parties

agree to consider such map and declaration as finally and conclusively fixing the said boundary.''

The same article further provided for a reference to a friendly sovereign or state, in the event of the commissioners being unable to agree.

The two governments appointed commissioners conformitory with this provision, namely, George III appointed on the part of Great Britain, Thomas Barclay, September 4, 1815, and President Madison appointed Cornelius Van Ness, April 3, 1816. Mr. Van Ness was a native of New York but at the time of his appointment resided in Vermont, and it appears that John Holmes, who was one of the commissioners to adjudicate in regard to the titles of the islands in Passamaquoddy Bay, also acted with them. Henry H. Orne was appointed secretary to this commission. Mr. Orne, who in the record was simply described as ''a citizen of the United States,'' was presumably Judge Henry Orne of Boston, from whom the town of Orneville in the county of Piscataquis derived its name.

This commission, after sitting for five years, could not even agree on a plan for a general map of the country exhibiting the boundaries respectively claimed by each party; much less could they settle any of the matters referred to them.

They accordingly dissolved and made separate reports to both governments, stating the points on which they differed, and the grounds of their difference.

Soon after the close of the War of 1812, settlements, not only in the northeastern parts of the Province of Maine, but in Nova Scotia and Quebec as well, began to increase; business was expanding and land under both flags was becoming more valuable.

All of these things tended to reawaken the interest in

the question of boundary lines between the two dominions.

Maine became a state in 1820, and by the Articles of Separation the Commonwealth of Massachusetts reserved to herself one half of the unincorporated lands within the Province of Maine.*

Hence not only the inhabitants of eastern Maine, but both of these states were intensely interested in having the matter decided.

Finally the statesmen of both governments concluded that a condition had arisen which made it necessary to refer the points of difference to a friendly sovereign under the terms of the treaty of Ghent; and on the 29th day of September, 1827, a convention to that effect was concluded.

Consequently in 1826, Albert Gallatin, who was one of the commissioners of the United States at Ghent in 1814, went to England as minister of the United States, charged with the duty of arranging various questions of difference and among them the North Eastern Boundary. He had many conferences with the plenipotentiaries representing that government, the principal result of which was the convention to refer the matter to a friendly sovereign under the provision of the treaty of Ghent herein before referred to.

The statements of the United States were prepared and submitted to the arbitrator by Mr. Gallatin who had associated with him Wm. Pitt Preble of Portland.†

---

*Act of Separation passed by Legislature of Massachusetts June 19, 1819, Sec. 1, part first.

†William P. Preble was a resident of Portland and was born in York, Me., November 27, 1783, and died October 11, 1857. He was graduated from Harvard College in 1806, studied law with Benjamin Hasey at Topsham and Mr. Orr in Brunswick. Practiced law in Alfred and Saco before he removed to Portland in 1818. In 1814 he

It was stipulated therein that Mitchell's map, by
which the framers of the treaty of 1783 had regulated
their joint and official proceedings, and a map denomi-
nated A, had been agreed upon by the contracting
parties, as a delineation of the water courses and a
general outline of the territory.

The King of the Netherlands was selected as arbiter
and when he heard the case of the high contracting
parties, changes of magnitude had taken place in both
the American and English possessions since the treaty of
1783.

The Province of Maine was independent from the
mother Commonwealth of Massachusetts and had entered
upon her career as a sovereign state of the Union.

Nova Scotia had been divided and a new province
erected called New Brunswick, within the borders of
which was the territory about which the contention had
arisen, and Quebec had been made into two provinces,
then known as Upper Canada and Lower Canada.

The task imposed upon the arbiter was an onerous one
but the duties were plain and not at all obscure.

He was to construe the provisions of the treaty of
1783, which related to this boundary, and make a decision which, if ratified by the two governments, would be
binding upon them.

This necessitated his making findings among other
things as to the following questions:

---

received the appointment of U. S. District Attorney from President
Madison.

In 1820 he was selected as one of the three judges composing the
highest judicial court of the new State of Maine.

In 1828 he resigned from the bench and entered upon diplomatic
service.

President Jackson appointed him Minister Plenipotentiary to The
Hague, and he was serving in this capacity when the King of Holland rendered his decision. He was in various ways active in the
affairs of the North Eastern Boundary question until its final settlement by the Webster-Ashburton treaty.

1. What was the "north-west angle of Nova Scotia?"
2. The "Source" of the St. Croix River?
3. What were the "Highlands," which "divide those rivers that empty themselves into the River St. Lawrence from those which fall into the Atlantic Ocean?"
4. What was the "Northwesternmost head of the Connecticut River?"

Incidental with, or subordinate to these were other questions which arose in the investigations and discussions as the case progressed before him, but I regard the foregoing as the principal or leading points in the controversy.

It was undoubtedly unfortunate for all parties to this imbroglio, that, in designating the northerly boundary between the territory of Massachusetts (Province of Maine) and Nova Scotia, in the treaty of 1783, the term "Highlands" should have been used. It was indefinite and susceptible of widely different construction. No writer has since maintained or even insinuated that the word was placed there by either party designedly or for any ulterior purpose.

It was without doubt, purely and simply, a case of careless and inconsiderate use of language. It should be observed that this word was not used in these treaties except in the sense of dividing rivers, and that in the early grants the intention of making the St. Lawrence River the northerly boundary of Maine seemed to be apparent.

This was the position taken by the American commissioners before the King of the Netherlands, and it was furthermore contended by them that, taking the whole article together, the word "Highlands" as therein expressed, referred to an unexplored country and was applicable to any ground, whatever might be its nature or elevation, along which the line dividing the rivers should be found to pass; and that the fact that the ground dividing rivers was necessarily more elevated than those rivers and their banks, was sufficient to entitle it to the designation of "Highlands" in relation to those rivers.

The United States claimed that a line from the source of the river St. Croix "directly north" reaches a ridge or "Highland" which divides tributary streams of the St. John River, which falls into the Bay of Fundy, from the waters of the Ristigouche River, which falls through the Bay des Chaleurs, into the Gulf of St. Lawrence; that this line crosses no other rivers for a distance exceeding ninety miles, but tributary streams of the St. John and that river itself. And furthermore that it was not necessary to find any continuous range of mountains, but continuous land which divided these rivers.

To be exact I copy the following from Gallatin's notes on the "American line" (page 17) which he compiled from the statements laid before the King of the Netherlands:

"At about ninety-seven miles from the source of the River St. Croix, the due north line reaches a ridge or Highland which divides tributary streams of the River St. John, which falls into the Bay of Fundy, from the waters of the River Ristigouche, which falls through the Bay des Chaleurs, into the Gulf of St. Lawrence. And, in its further north course, the said line, after crossing several upper branches of the River Ristigouche, reaches, at the distance of about 140 miles from the source of the River St. Croix the Highlands, which divide the waters of the said River Ristigouche from the tributary streams of the River Metis, which falls into the River St. Lawrence. It is clear that there is no other possible choice but between those two places, and that the northwest angle of Nova Scotia must, of necessity, be found at the intersection of the said due north line with, either the Highlands which divide the waters of the River St. John from those of the River Ristigouche, or the Highlands which divide the waters of the River Ristigouche from those of the River Metis; since there is no other point, through the whole course of the due north line, which divides any other waters but such as empty themselves into the same river.

"The selection between those two dividing Highlands evidently depends on what is meant, according to the treaty of 1783, by rivers that empty themselves or fall into the River St. Lawrence, and by rivers which fall into the Atlantic Ocean.

"The treaty recognizes but two classes of rivers. The first class embraces only the rivers falling into a river, designated by its specific name, and cannot be construed to include any rivers that do not empty themselves into the river thus specially designated. All the rivers, met by the due north line, which do not actually empty themselves into the River St. Lawrence, according to its known limits, are, by the treaty, considered as falling into the Atlantic Ocean."

The British theory from first to last was that "Highlands" represented a mountainous or hilly country or district.

They would not admit its American significance as a continuous line dividing rivers regardless of whether such line was mountainous or not.

There may have been some reason for this as they had been familiar with the term as applied to a region of Highlands in Scotland which distinguished it from the Lowlands, Etc.

Their writers from time immemorial had thus described sections which were of high elevation and had not generally used the word in the American sense as a dividing line, a ridge or a range.

In the same notes (page 18) Mr. Gallatin says:

"It is denied on the part of Great Britain, that the boundary thus claimed by the United States, is that which is prescribed or intended by the treaty principally, if not exclusively, on two grounds:

"1st. That the Bay of Fundy, as mentioned in the treaty of 1783, is, (as well as the Gulf of St. Lawrence,) intended to be separate and distinct from the Atlantic Ocean; and that the River St. John, which falls into the Bay of Fundy, (as well as the River Ristigouche which, through the Bay des Chaleurs, falls into the Gulf of St. Lawrence,) is intended, on that as well as on separate grounds, to be excepted from that class of rivers which are described in the treaty as falling into the Atlantic Ocean.

"2ndly. That the ground over which the boundary line claimed by the United States does pass, has neither the mountainous character, nor the continuous elevation necessary to entitle it to the designation of 'Highlands,' as intended by the treaty; and therefore, that the Highlands, claimed on the part of the United States, conform neither in position or character, to the conditions imposed on them by the treaty.

"From those premises, and with reference particularly to the assertion, that the River St. John must be excepted from that class of rivers described in the treaty as falling into the Atlantic Ocean, it is inferred, on the part of Great Britain, that, consequently the Highlands described in the treaty must lie to the southward of that River. And it is further affirmed, that the Highlands, claimed, on the part of Great Britain, as those designated in the treaty of 1783, conform, in every particular, to the conditions imposed on them by that treaty."

The north line would terminate at Mars Hill as the British construed the treaty, while under the American construction it would run as far north as the sources of the Ristigouche River, which empties into the Bay des Chaleurs.

The St. John River was midway between the two lines, or in about the central part of the disputed territory.

Had the British claim prevailed, all of what is now Aroostook County, north of Mars Hill, and the most of what is now Piscataquis County, northerly of the Penobscot waters, would be a part of Canada; and if the Americans had finally been sustained in all that they contended for, the rich St. John River valley and a large stretch of territory northerly, easterly and northwesterly would now be a part of the State of Maine.

For the purpose of this sketch it is not necessary to consider the numerous subjects which were involved when the case was tried out before the arbiter. Thirty or more maps published in London subsequent to the proclamation of 1763, were among the exhibits placed before him by the United States, eighteen of which were published before the treaty of 1783.

The English made the point that the negotiators of the treaty of 1783 had no evidence before them of the actual geography of the country, and hence the words of the treaty were not effectual, and yet these last-named eighteen maps all made plain the situation of the basin of the St. John, the sources of the Penobscot, which were rivers and streams falling into the Atlantic, and those of the tributary streams of the St. Lawrence.

The negotiators of that treaty had access to these maps and made use of them, consequently the Americans contended that the highland or ridge of land which divided these tributary streams, was the "Highlands" described in the treaty, and that it constituted a well-defined boundary line which could be found upon the face of the earth, and that there was no reason whatever for assuming that when those words were mutually written into the treaty their significance and meaning were not fully understood.

It would seem that the gist of the entire issue before the King of the Netherlands was, what were the intentions of the negotiators of the treaty of 1783, and it is difficult to perceive just how any acts of jurisdiction subsequently exercised by either party over the contested territory, could have thrown any light on these intentions or affected in any manner the terms of the treaty.

And yet both sides were allowed to and did present evidence of this nature, some of which is interesting even though its materiality at that time may be doubted.

It appeared that in the year 1784, a native Indian was tried and convicted by a court of the Province of Quebec, and accordingly executed for a murder committed, as was suggested, on the waters of the river St. John; that between the years, 1789 and 1791, two suits were instituted and judgment obtained, before the courts of Quebec by some inhabitants of Canada against persons residing on the river Madawaska; that an extract from a list of the parishes in the Province of Quebec, taken from the minutes of the Executive Council for 1791, includes that of Madawaska,* and that, in the year

---

*A part of the disputed territory was during the entire controversy over the North Eastern Boundary, known as Madawaska. Upon a part of this is now situated the town of Madawaska in the State of Maine. This territory was anciently called the Fief of Madawaska; the original concession of it having been made by the Government of Canada to the children of the Sieur Charles Auburt de la Chenaye, November 25, 1683. This concession contained the following condition:

"Subject to the Foi et hommage, which the grantees, their heirs

1785, that council issued an order for opening a road from Kamarouska on the river St. Lawrence to Lake Temisquata, which lies on the southeastern side of the dividing Highlands, claimed as their boundary by the United States.

Seldom has an international question been so thoroughly discussed as was that of this disputed boundary.*

---

and assigns, shall he holden to render at the Castle of St. Louis of Quebec of which they are to hold, and subject to the customary rights and dues in conformity with the Contume de Paris.''

By an adjudication of the Prevotal Court of Quebec, dated October 29th, 1709, this Seigniory of Madawaska was seized by virtue of a sentence of that court and was sold to Joseph Blondeau dit la Franchise as the highest bidder at a public judicial sale for the sum of 1,300 livres, and was accordingly adjudged to the said Joseph Blondeau.

On the 15th day of February, 1723, it appears, by some kind of a judicial proceeding or report, that ''on the Fief of Madawaska there was a domain, on which the buildings had been burnt by the Indians, and that there were six 'arpens' of land cleared, but at that time no settlement.''

By an adjudication by the Prevotal Court of Quebec, dated July 29th, 1755, founded on what was called a ''voluntary judicial sale,'' Madawaska passed to Pierre Claverie. After Canada became a part of the dominion of Great Britain by conquest, the title to this territory passed by judicial sale to Richard Murray and on August 2, 1768, by deed of assignment by Richard Murray to Malcolm Fraser.

The latest deed of Madawaska under these titles that we have evidence of was dated August 2, 1802, but between this and the last named date there had been several transfers by judicial sale and otherwise.

This chain of titles was introduced before the King of the Netherlands, by the British commissioners, to show continuous possession and ownership by Great Britain to Madawaska. The reply of the United States to this contention was, that since the conquest no one had performed acts of fealty and homage under the condition of the original concession of 1683, and hence the title had been forfeited and abandoned by reason of the failure to comply with these feudal services.

(Appendix to the first British Statement before the King of the Netherlands.)

---

*History and Digest of International Arbitrations, Vol. I, p. 91.

Gallatin asserted that he devoted nearly two years in studying and preparing the case, and bestowed on it more time than he ever did on any other question.*

Finally on the 10th day of January, 1831, the decision of the King of the Netherlands was made public and it was a surprise to both governments and to all parties of interest.

When his award was analyzed, it was found that he had sustained in words the American contention that the term "Highlands" was applicable to ground which, without being mountainous or hilly, divided rivers flowing in the opposite directions; but that it was not shown that the boundaries described in the treaty of 1783 coincided with the ancient limits of the British provinces; and that neither the line of Highlands claimed by Great Britain so nearly answered the requirements of the treaty of 1783 in respect to division of rivers as to give preference one over the other.

Abandoning therefore the attempt to determine this part of the boundary according to the treaty of 1783, he recommended what was termed a line of "convenience"† or in other words, he made an arbitrary line, not found in Mitchell's map, Map A, or in any of the maps used by the negotiators of the treaty of 1783, of the treaty of Ghent, or by either party before him.

It was evidently intended by him as a compromise, pure and simple.

On the 12th day of January, 1831, Mr. Preble, who was then envoy-extraordinary of the United States at The Hague, addressed to the British Minister of Foreign Affairs, a note, respectfully protesting against the award and reserving the rights and interests of the

*Adams' Writings of Gallatin, Vol. II, p. 549.

†History and Digest of International Arbitrations, Vol. I, p. 136.

United States on the ground that the proceedings of the arbitrator constituted a departure from his powers.

Mr. Preble also took the ground that the object of the arbitration was to have executed the terms of the treaty of 1783 and that if this could not be done, the question of boundaries ought never again be submitted to any sovereign. And he thus formally entered his protest against the proceedings.

The British government, while apparently not satisfied with the award, expressed its acquiescence in it, but authorized its minister privately to intimate to the United States that it would not consider the formal acceptance of the award as precluding modifications of the line by mutual exchange and consideration.

The government at Washington for a time hesitated as to what course to pursue. Mr. Preble's protest had been entered without instructions from his government and President Jackson was at first inclined to accept the award.

As the action of the King of the Netherlands became more fully understood by the people of Maine and Massachusetts, its discussion by newspapers and public men became bitter and its criticism more and more intense; and the President's political enemies in both states were severely blaming him for his procrastination in the matter.

At one time he was disposed to issue a proclamation, accepting of the terms of the award without consulting the Senate, but was driven from this course by his political friends in Maine, who represented to him that such a course would change the politics of the State.*

It is said that he regretted in after years that he did

*Webster's Works, Vol. 1, p. 119.

not follow out his own inclinations in regard to the subject.*

President Jackson therefore submitted the question of acceptance or rejection to the Senate on the 7th day of December, 1831, and in June, 1832, the award was rejected by a vote of 35 to 8, and the Senate at the same time advised the President to open a new negotiation with Great Britain for the ascertainment of the line.

The British government promised to enter upon the negotiations in a friendly spirit; and it was stipulated and agreed that both sides should refrain from exercising any jurisdiction beyond the boundaries which they actually possessed.

Meanwhile the government of the United States made earnest though unsuccessful attempts to obtain from the State of Maine full authority to adjust the matter with Great Britain.

The proposition was for Maine to provisionally surrender to the Federal government all of her right to the disputed territory for the purpose of a settlement.

These offers were, however, all rejected by the State of Maine and then the British government formally withdrew its offer to accept the compromise recommended by the King of the Netherlands.

No real progress was made and nothing accomplished towards a settlement of the controversy during the remainder of President Jackson's administration.

President Van Buren sent a message to the Senate March 20, 1838, with recent correspondence about the subject between the Secretary of State, Mr. Forsyth, and the British Minister, Mr. Fox.

Mr. Forsyth recommended a new conventional line, or another submission to arbitration and the President in

*Webster's Works, Vol. 1, p. 119.

his message expressed the hope that "an early and satisfactory adjustment of it could be effected."

Governor Kent submitted the question to the Legislature of Maine, which body on the 23d day of March, 1838, resolved that it was not expedient to assent to the Federal government's treating for a conventional line, but that the State should insist on the line established by the treaty of 1783, and that the senators and representatives in Congress be requested to urge the passage of a bill then pending for a survey of the boundary.

In 1839, Messrs. Featherstonhaugh and Mudge, employed by the English authorities, surveyed a part of the line and the government at Washington provided for a survey in 1840.

Nothing of importance resulted from either of these surveys.

For a decade of years subsequent to the award of the King of the Netherlands it was a theme of vast interest to the people of Maine and of Massachusetts as well.

The General Court of that commonwealth made various reports regarding it at different times. The Governors of Maine discussed it in their messages and the Legislature made several exhaustive reports upon it.

Indissolubly interwoven with this controversy is the arrest, imprisonment and punishment of one John Baker, a resident of what was known as the Madawaska Settlement.

The rights of the Commonwealth of Massachusetts to Madawaska and adjacent lands on the Aroostook River were recognized at an early period after the source of the St. Croix was settled by the convention of 1794.

Grants were accordingly made by the Legislature of Massachusetts of lots of land embracing both branches of the Aroostook River* and bordering on the boundary

---

*This river was originally known as "Restook" and "Ristook."

line, namely: One to the town of Plymouth and one to General Eaton.

Locations and surveys of these lands were made under authority of Massachusetts.

Among other grants was that of a lot of land to John Baker "of a plantation called and known by the name of Madawaska Settlement, in the County of Penobscot, and State of Maine," the deed of which was executed jointly by "George W. Coffin, agent for the Commonwealth of Massachusetts, and James Irish, agent for the State of Maine," on the third day of October, 1825. Another deed of land situated below Baker's was made to James Bacon.

Baker had a farm and a small store, and also a grist and sawmill. Other settlers soon became his neighbors and his place was a center and headquarters for the American settlers in that locality.

One George Morehouse resided in Tobique, in a parish then recently formed and known as Kent.

He held a magistrate's commission from the Province of New Brunswick, and the first of the Madawaska troubles seem to have arisen from a practice which he had instituted as magistrate, although there is no evidence that he was in the first instance in any way authorized or instructed by the province authorities to pursue it.

This was no less a procedure than issuing precepts directed to the constables of the Parish of Kent, for the recovery of small demands against the inhabitants along the Aroostook River.

Criminal processes against these inhabitants were also occasionally issued by Magistrate Morehouse.

The serving of these precepts was often resisted by them and sometimes by force.

That Baker was a leader among these settlers is true and that he may have advised them to thus resist the officers which he believed had no authority or jurisdiction there, is also undoubtedly a fact.

Thus the strife between Morehouse and his followers on the one hand, and the American settlers, led by Baker, on the other hand, continually increased until it seemed to have culminated some time in the early fall of 1827 by an incident which now seems more amusing than tragic.

The Americans had erected a staff, or what might have been known as a "liberty pole," although it does not appear that they had any flag, and upon the top of it had attached a rude representation of the American Eagle.

The Americans had occasional gatherings and festivities around this national emblem, which it may be imagined, were more or less convivial, and they sometimes jeered and perhaps annoyed passers-by from the province who acknowledged allegiance to the Sovereign of England.

When Morehouse learned of this he became enraged and called upon Baker and ordered him to remove it. This Baker refused to do, whereupon Morehouse procured a subpœna from Thomas Wetmore, Esq., attorney-general of New Brunswick, dated September 17, 1827, for his arrest.

Early in the morning of September 25th, while Baker and his family were asleep, his house was surrounded by an armed force and he was arrested and taken before Magistrate Morehouse,* who committed him to the jail in

*Report of Charles S. Davies to the Governor of Maine, January 31, 1831, p. 29. There may be some doubt however about this statement as the subpœna commanded him to appear before the court in Fredericton.

Fredericton without even examination or trial, if the accounts of the transaction published at the time are to be believed.

But while Morehouse may or may not have been incited by the New Brunswick authorities to do these unlawful acts, they were themselves responsible for some things equally as illegal, among which was that of assessing and levying a special and wholly illegal tax upon these settlers which was known as the "Alien tax."*

Baker was prosecuted at various times and one of the alleged grounds for action against him and for several other similar proceedings against Americans in Madawaska and along the Aroostook River was, that they were trespassers on crown lands. Lumber that had been sawed at Baker's mill was seized and confiscated while being transported down the St. John.

Magistrate Morehouse seems to have spent considerable time in harassing the settlers on the Aroostook in devious ways.

Early in the spring of 1827 he assumed to have authority to prevent them from working on the lands which they occupied, and forbade their doing so, and also posted up written notices to this effect on the Eaton Grant, and in different places; and marked some small piles of timber which they had cut, for seizure.†

He did not even treat them as English subjects but apparently regarded them as outlaws and intruders without a country, and without rights which anyone was bound to respect.

In July, 1827, Daniel Craig, a deputy sheriff of the Parish of Kent, who was sent by Morehouse, delivered summonses to all of the inhabitants to appear before the

---

*Gov. Lincoln's letter to the Secretary of State of the United States, September 3, 1827.

†Davies' Report, p. 10.

court in Fredericton in pleas of trespass and intrusion on crown lands.*

This sudden and unexpected proceeding naturally created a state of consternation and alarm.

The precepts were served only a few days before the court was to convene. Some went to Fredericton only to learn that the cases were delayed until the next winter. Some went part way and then returned home, while many did not heed the summonses at all.

It was said that those who did go suffered much hardship as they were far from home without means of sustenance.

One man, James Armstrong, was seized in the house of his brother, Ferdinand Armstrong, placed in a canoe and forcibly deported beyond the territory.†

Their market was at Houlton and their only means of transportation was down the St. John River, but as their produce was often seized while en route and as they were subject to so much oppression from the provincial officers, in the fall and winter of 1827-8 they determined to cut out a woods road to Houlton which should be wholly on undisputed American soil.

The first attempt at this was a failure as the explorers who were employed to "spot" out the road, lost their way and after much suffering and privation, found themselves in Foxcroft.‡

It is evident that these American settlers desired to live quiet and peaceful lives, for the means which they resorted to to circumvent provincial authority fully demonstrate this.

When they had endured the methods and practices of Morehouse and others as long as they felt it was possible,

*Davies' Report, p. 11.
†Ib. p. 12.
‡Ib. p. 12.

instead of organizing an armed revolt which might have been natural under the circumstances, they conceived the idea of a general agreement to avoid all resort to courts or legal proceedings whatever.

The plan was simple and yet unique and perhaps in a degree communistic.

A paper was accordingly drawn up and signed by the American inhabitants generally, constituting a sort of compact, by which they mutually agreed to adjust all disputes of whatever nature which might arise among themselves, by virtue of referees, without admission of British authority, and that they would support each other in abiding by this determination.

This was to be a provisional agreement, to continue in force only for one year; and, in the meantime, application was to be made to the government, in order to obtain, if possible, the benefit of some regular authority.*

Thus these isolated and primitive people in that desolate and remote region, buffeted by the persecutions of one government, and forsaken and abandoned to their own resources by another government, more than half a century after the treaty of 1783, proposed to free themselves from the tyranny of all magistrates, courts, lawyers and officers.

This paper or written agreement among the inhabitants of Madawaska, was, as will hereafter appear, one of the grounds for the indictment against Baker and others for alleged conspiracy and sedition.

The redoubtable Morehouse, as might have been anticipated, appeared upon the scene as soon as he learned of the existence of this written agreement and demanded it of them, but it was in their estimation, too sacred a document to part with, and they refused to

---

*Davies' Report, p. 23.

deliver it up as did the people of Connecticut refuse to surrender their ancient charter to James II in 1687.

At the Hilary term* of the Supreme Court in 1828, the grand jury for the County of York in the Province of New Brunswick found a true bill of indictment against John Baker, James Bacon and Charles Studson, for conspiracy.

The defendants, Bacon and Studson, were never taken into custody, but John Baker was arrested and arraigned Thursday, May 8, 1828, before the Honorable Chief Justice Saunders, Mr. Justice Bliss and Mr. Justice Chipman.

The indictment alleged that the defendants "being persons greatly disaffected to our said lord the now King, and his Government, within this his Majesty's Province of New Brunswick, and being factiously and seditiously disposed, on the fourth day of July in the eighth year of the reign of our said Sovereign Lord George the Fourth, with force and arms, at the parish aforesaid, in the county aforesaid, did amongst themselves, conspire, combine, confederate, and agree together, falsely, maliciously, factiously, and seditiously, and to bring hatred and contempt on our said lord the King, etc, etc."

The first overt act complained of in this indictment was that on the said fourth day of July at the place above named, the defendants "in pursuance of, and according to said conspiracy," * * * * did "cause to be raised and erected, a certain flag-staff, and did place thereon a certain flag, as the Standard of the United States of America."

---

*Hilary Term. In English law. A term of court, beginning on the 11th and ending on the 31st of January in each year. Superseded (1875) by Hilary sittings, which begin January 11th, and end on the Wednesday before Easter.

The second overt act relates to the provisional paper which the inhabitants had signed as above referred to and alleged that the defendants had "applied to divers liege subjects of our said lord the King, and then and there presented to the same subjects a paper writing, which they the said John Baker, James Bacon and Charles Studson, then and there requested the said subjects to sign, then and there declaring that, by the said paper, they the said subjects, would bind themselves to oppose the execution of the laws of Great Britain, to wit, in the Madawaska settlement, so called."

The third overt act states that the defendants "did oppose and obstruct the post man" in carrying the mail through Madawaska settlement, etc.

The attorney general appeared and prosecuted the case for the crown while the defendant Baker appeared without counsel and defended himself during the trial. Baker was found guilty, and sentenced to two months imprisonment, and to pay a fine of £25 to the king.

Prior to the arrest of Baker he and James Bacon had been selected by the inhabitants as "a deputation" to proceed to the seat of government of Maine with a request to have their case laid before the Legislature at its next session ; and to enquire of the executive authority whether they were recognized as citizens of the State of Maine and entitled to its protection.

These two men attended to this duty by traveling on foot and by canoe much of the way ; they then "returned through the wilderness by the way they came."

One of the results of their mission was the following proclamation by the Governor of Maine:

"Whereas it has been made known to this State, that one of its citizens has been conveyed from it, by a Foreign Power, to a gaol in the Province of New Brunswick ; and that many trespasses have been committed by inhabitants of the same Province upon the sovereignty of Maine and the rights of those she is bound to protect.

"Be it also known, that, relying on the government and people of the Union, the proper exertion will be applied to obtain reparation and security.

"Those, therefore, suffering wrong, or threatened with it, and those interested by sympathy, on account of the violation of our territory and immunities, are exhorted to forbearance and peace, so that the preparations for preventing the removal of our land marks, and guarding the sacred and inestimable rights of American citizens may not be embarrassed by any unauthorized acts.

ENOCH LINCOLN.

Portland, November 9, 1827."

The Legislature of 1828 also passed this resolve:

"Whereas the sovereignty of this State has been repeatedly violated by the acts of the agents and officers of the Government of the British Province of New Brunswick, and that government, by its agents and officers, has wantonly and injuriously harassed the citizens of this State, residing on the North Eastern frontier of the same, and within its limits, by assuming to exercise jurisdiction over them, in issuing and executing civil and criminal process against them, by which their property has been seized, and some of them arrested and conveyed out of the State, and subjected to the operation of the laws of that Province; and in establishing military companies within the territory of this State; imposing fines for neglect of military duty; imposing upon our said citizens an alien tax, and requiring payment of the same; and Whereas, by the exercise of the aforesaid unwarranted acts of jurisdiction by the govern-

ment of the said Province, some of our citizens have
been deprived of their liberty, their property destroyed,
many of them driven from their lands and dwellings,
the tranquility and peace of all of them disturbed, and
the settlement and population of that part of the State
adjoining said Province, greatly retarded, if not wholly
prevented: Therefore,

"RESOLVED, That the present is a crisis, in which
the government and people of this State, have good
cause to look to the government of the United States
for defence and protection against foreign aggression.

"RESOLVED FURTHER, That if new aggressions
shall be made by the government of the Province of
New-Brunswick upon the territory of this State, and
upon its citizens, and seasonable protection shall not be
given by the United States, the Governor be, and he
hereby is requested to use all proper and constitutional
means in his power, to protect and defend the citizens
aforesaid in the enjoyment of their rights.

"RESOLVED FURTHER, That, in the opinion of
this Legislature, the Executive of the United States
ought, without delay, to demand of the British Government the immediate restoration of John Baker, a citizen
of this State, who has been seized by the officers of the
Province of New Brunswick, within the territory of the
State of Maine, and by them conveyed to Fredericton,
in said Province, where he is now confined in prison; and
to take such measures as will effect his early release.

"RESOLVED FURTHER, That the Governor be,
and he hereby is, authorized and requested, with the
advice and consent of Council, from time to time, to
extend to the family of the said John Baker, such relief
as shall be deemed necessary; and he is hereby authorized to draw his warrant on the Treasury for such sum
or sums as shall be required for that purpose.

In the House of Representatives, Feb. 16, 1828.
Read and passed,
JOHN RUGGLES, Speaker.
Attest, James L. Child, Clerk.
In Senate, February 18, 1828,
Read and passed,
ROBERT P. DUNLAP, President.
Attest, Ebenezer Hutchinson, Sec'y.
February 18, 1828—Approved,
ENOCH LINCOLN.''

In 1831 the attempt of certain persons to hold an election at Madawaska Settlement under the laws of Maine, led to their arrest and trial by the authorities of New Brunswick.

They were convicted and sentenced to fine and imprisonment, but were afterwards released on the request of the United States government, their action having been disavowed by the authorities of Maine.

In June, 1837, Ebenezer Greeley of Dover, Maine, was employed by the State of Maine as an agent to take the census of the people of Madawaska, and at the same time, to distribute their share of the surplus money which had accumulated in the United States Treasury.*

A provincial constable arrested Mr. Greeley and carried him as a prisoner to Fredericton, N. B.

But while the Fredericton officials had for some time unhesitatingly imprisoned humble and uninfluential citizens of Maine when brought to them in custody, they were alarmed at this bold procedure. The sheriff there feared to detain in gaol an agent or officer of the State of Maine while in the discharge of his duties, and refused to receive the prisoner. After being liberated,

*Abbot's History of Maine, p. 431.

Mr. Greeley returned to the Aroostook and resumed his labors as census taker.

In a short time after this, however, Governor Harvey of New Brunswick, hearing that Mr. Greeley was distributing money to the people,* assumed, without making any attempt to obtain evidence of the facts, that it was done as a bribe to induce the inhabitants to continue their allegiance to the United States.

He therefore ordered Mr. Greeley to be rearrested, and he was lodged in Fredericton jail.†

Governor Dunlap of Maine issued a general order announcing that the soil of the State had been invaded by a foreign power and the militia was called upon to hold itself in readiness for momentary and active service.

A few weeks later, the British authorities, influenced by a message from President Van Buren, again liberated Mr. Greeley, who once more returned to the turbulent Aroostook and remained there until he had completed his services.‡

That the people of the new State of Maine were actuated by a spirit of patriotism, in vigorously opposing the encroachment of the officials of the Province of New Brunswick, upon what they believed to be their territory; that the feeling, when the District of Maine was separated from the Commonwealth of Massachusetts, in 1820, and admitted into the Union of States, was intense and increased year by year, as they saw what they deemed to be their unquestioned rights, trampled upon by the

---

*This was the famous "distribution of the surplus" under Pres. Jackson which was one of the most notable events of his administration.

†Abbot's History of Maine, p. 431.

‡Mr. Greeley was released "without trial or explanation and returned to his home." (Message of Gov. Kent, 1839.)

province, supported and protected by Great Britain, was bitter and uncompromising, is true.

William King, the first Governor of Maine, in his message to the Legislature, June 2, 1820, refers to the importance of the North Eastern Boundary question, to both Maine and Massachusetts.

Governor Paris, in 1822, expressed "great anxiety," because of the disagreement of the commissioners, under the treaty of Ghent, "in relation to the true boundary, between the United States and the British Provinces," and he again referred to it in his message, in 1824.

In 1825, he also called attention to it, and to the fact "that depredations, to a very considerable extent, have been committed on our timber lands, lying on the Aroostook and Mawascah and other streams," and that "these depredations were committed by British Subjects."

And in 1826, a considerable part of his annual message is devoted to this subject.

On January 17, 1826, the Joint Standing Committee on State Lands, made a report to the Legislature, relative to the boundary question accompanied by the following resolve, which received a passage:

"Resolved, That the Governor, for the time being, be authorized and requested to take such measures as he may think expedient and effectual, to procure for the use of the State, copies of all such maps, documents, publications, papers and surveys, relating to the North Eastern Boundary of the United States, described in the treaty of 1783, and such other information on that subject, as he may deem necessary and useful for this State to be possessed of; and that the sum of five hundred dollars be appropriated to carry into effect the provisions of this Resolve; and that the Governor be authorized to draw his warrants on the treasury for the same, as occasion, from time to time, may require, he to be accountable for the same.

"Resolved, That the Governor of this State, in conjunction with the Governor of the Commonwealth of Massachusetts, (provided said Commonwealth shall concur in the measure,) be authorized to cause the Eastern and Northern lines of the State of Maine to be explored, and the monuments, upon those lines, mentioned in the treaty of 1783, to be ascertained in such manner as may be deemed most expedient."

In 1829, Gov. Lincoln said in his message, "that the decision of the dispute, as to our North Eastern Boundary, is referred to the King of the Netherlands, and while I submit that no reference in such a case, was warrantable, yet there seems to be no objection to the personage selected, for how can he, the subject of impartial history, and not apparently dependent on any advantage from either party, being an umpire between nations, act but as the magnanimous dispenser of justice, who has the power to achieve the most glorious victory by the suppression of the most extreme error?"

When the Legislature of Maine convened, in 1831, the King of the Netherlands had rendered his decision.

An official communication from President Van Buren _Jackson,_ to Governor Smith, together with a translation of the full text of the award, was transmitted to the Legislature, with a special message by the Governor, who had also devoted a considerable portion of his annual message to the matter.

A joint select committee was appointed by the Legislature to consider the whole subject, who submitted an elaborate and exhaustive report, full of indignation at the findings of the arbitrator, signed by its chairman, John G. Deane.

It not only attacked the impartiality of the arbitrator, but strongly intimated, that he was not in fact, a sovereign, within the true meaning of the convention, which clothed him with the power and authority to act.

These resolutions closed as follows:

"Whereas, By the convention of September, 1827, an independent sovereign was to be selected by the governments of the United States and Great Britain, to arbitrate and settle such disputes as had arisen, and the King of the Netherlands was pursuant to that convention selected the arbiter, while an independent sovereign, in the plentitude of his power, exercising dominion and authority over more than 6,000,000 of subjects:

"And Whereas, By the force of the prevalence of liberal opinions in Belgium, the Belgians overthrew his power and deprived him of more than half of his dominions and reduced him to the former dominions of the Stadtholder, leaving him with the empty title of the King of the Netherlands while he is only the King of Holland, and thereby increasing his dependence upon Great Britain for holding his power even in Holland, which from Public appearances, he held from a very doubtful tenure in the affections of the Dutch.

"And Whereas, The King of the Netherlands had not decided before his Kingdom was dismembered and he consented to the division, and his public character had changed, so that he had ceased to be that public character, and occupying that independent station among the sovereigns of Europe contemplated by the convention of September, 1827, and which led to his selection.

"Therefore Resolved in the opinion of this Legislature, That the decision of the King of the Netherlands, cannot and ought not to be considered obligatory upon the government of the United States, either on the principles of right and justice, or of honor.

"Resolved Further—for the reasons before stated, That no decision made by any umpire under any circumstances, if the decision dismembers a state, has or can have, any constitutional force or obligation upon the State thus dismembered unless the State adopt and sanction the decision."

At the session of the Legislature of 1831, an act was passed to incorporate the town of Madawaska, including territory southward of the river St. John, and the disputed territory northward* of that river.

In 1832, Governor Smith, in his annual message said:

"In the month of October last, information was received that a number of the inhabitants of Madawaska had organized themselves into a corporation, chosen municipal officers, and subsequently a representative; and that in consequence of these acts, the lieutenant-governor and other authorities of New Brunswick, accompanied with a military force, had proceeded to Madawaska, and arrested a number of American citizens, who were carried to Fredericton, and there imprisoned.

"Though the measures adopted by the inhabitants, voluntarily organizing themselves into a corporation at that place, then claimed to be under the actual jurisdiction of the Province of New Brunswick, were unexpected by me, and undertaken without my knowledge; yet, as they acted in territory known to be within the limits of Maine, and in obedience to the laws and constitution, I considered that they were entitled to the aid and protection of their government.

"Immediately, therefore, on receiving evidence of these transactions, they were communicated, together with all the circumstances in relation to them within my knowledge, to the Department of State of the United

---

*Now Upper Madawaska in the Province of New Brunswick.

States, with a request that the proper measures might be adopted by the General Government to procure the release of our citizens, and to protect the territory of our State from invasion. Upon the receipt of this communication, though the proceedings of the inhabitants of Madawaska were considered to be a breach of the arrangement made with the British Minister, for preserving the state of things as it then existed on both sides, till a final disposition of the question, those measures were promptly adopted by the President, which resulted in the release of our citizens from imprisonment, and rendered further proceedings on the part of this State, in reference to that object, unnecessary.''

A special committee was appointed, to which was referred that part of Governor Smith's message that related to the North Eastern Boundary. Among its members appear the names of Reuel Williams and Nathan Clifford. They submitted the following resolves:

"Resolved, That the Constitution of the United States does not invest the General Government with unlimited and absolute powers, but confers only a special and modified sovereignty, without authority to cede to a foreign power any portion of territory belonging to a State, without its consent.

"Resolved, That if there is any attribute of State Sovereignty which is unqualified and undeniable, it is the right of jurisdiction to the utmost limits of State Territory; and if a single obligation under the constitution rests upon the Confederacy, it is to guarantee the integrity of this territory to the quiet and undisturbed enjoyment of the States.

"Resolved, That the doings of the King of Holland, on the subject of the boundary between the United States and Great Britain, are not a decision of the question submitted to the King of the Netherlands; and that his recommendation of a suitable or convenient line of boundary is not obligatory upon the parties to the submission.

"Resolved, That this State protests against the adoption, by the Government of the United States, of the line of boundary recommended by the King of Holland as a suitable boundary between Great Britain and the United States; inasmuch as it will be a violation of the rights of Maine,—rights acknowledged and insisted upon by the General Government,—and will be a precedent which endangers the integrity, as well as the independence, of every State in the Union.

"Resolved, That while the people of this State are disposed to yield a ready obedience to the Constitution and laws of the United States, they will never consent to surrender any portion of their territory, on the recommendation of a foreign power.

"Resolved, That the Governor, with advice of Council, be authorized to appoint a competent agent, whose duty it shall be, as soon as may be, to repair to the City of Washington, and deliver to the President of the United States a copy of the preceding Report and these Resolutions, with a request that he will lay the same before the Senate of the United States; and also deliver a copy to the Vice President, to each of the Heads of Departments, and to each member of the Senate, and to our Representative in Congress.

"Resolved, That our Senators in Congress be instructed, and our Representatives requested, to use their best efforts to prevent our State from being dismembered, our territory alienated, and our just rights prostrated, by the adoption of a new line for our North Eastern Boundary, as recommended by the King of Holland.

"Resolved, That the agent to be appointed by the Governor and Council, be instructed to cooperate with our Senators and Representatives, in advocating and enforcing the principles advanced, and positions taken, in the foregoing Resolutions, and in supporting all such measures as shall be deemed best calculated to preserve the integrity of our State, and prevent any portion of our territory and citizens from being transferred to a Foreign Power."

Governor Dunlap, in 1834, notes that this question is still unsettled, but considers that the way "is now open for the ultimate attainment of our rights," inasmuch that the President of the United States had announced as the policy of the national administration, in negotiations with foreign powers, to "submit to nothing that is wrong."

In the years 1834, 1835 and 1836 the Governors' messages refer to it only as "yet being in an unsettled state," but in 1837, Governor Dunlap regrets that he has "received no information to warrant the opinion that a speedy adjustment is expected," and asserts that "our soil and our sovereignty have been invaded."

A joint committee at this session of the Legislature was appointed to investigate and report. John Holmes was its chairman on the part of the House.

Their report of ten pages was one of the most searching that had been made, and they submitted the following resolutions:

"Resolved, That we view with much solicitude the British usurpations and encroachments on the northeastern part of the territory of this State.

"Resolved, That pretensions so groundless and extravagant indicate a spirit of hostility which we had no reason to expect from a nation with whom we are at peace.

"Resolved, That vigilance, resolution, firmness and union on the part of this State, are necessary in this state of the controversy.

"Resolved, That the Governor be authorized and requested to call on the President of the United States to cause the North Eastern Boundary of this State to be explored and surveyed and monuments erected according to the Treaty of 1783.

"Resolved, That the cooperation of Massachusetts be requested.

"Resolved, That our Senators in Congress be instructed, and our Representatives requested to endeavor to obtain a speedy adjustment of the controversy.

"Resolved, That copies of this report and resolutions be transmitted to the Governor of Massachusetts, the President of the United States, to each of our Senators and Representatives in Congress and other Senators in Congress, and the Governors of the several States."

When the Legislature of 1838 had assembled, the people of Maine had become exasperated, for since the adjournment of the last Legislature, the depredations and trespasses upon territory that was in dispute, also upon portions of territory to which the title of Maine was practically undisputed, had increased to an alarming degree.

The province people, evidently fully supported by their officials and the government of Great Britain, had never before been so arrogant, defiant and insolent in extending by force and unlawful means, their alleged jurisdictional rights, as during the years then drawing to a close. The conditions were acute and the situation serious.

The Whigs had gained the ascendancy in Maine and had elected Edward Kent, governor. Governor Kent was an able lawyer and a profound jurist, and was for many years after, one of the ablest, members of the Supreme Court of this State. He had informed himself fully of the complex conditions and had given the whole matter careful consideration, hence, his elaboration of it in his annual message is such a lucid history of the events to that time, and the rights of Maine as viewed from a conservative and judicial standpoint, that copious extracts are herein made from it. Among other things he said :

"Constitutional Law is the broad and ample shield under which a whole people rest in security and peace. Like the atmosphere in which we move, it presses with immense, but equal and balanced power, to sustain the body politic. It protects the infant in its cradle and the magistrate in the seat of Justice. It gives the consciousness of security and safety to the unarmed and the peaceful, and is more than bolts and bars in guarding every man's castle—his own domestic hearth. The weak fear not the strength of the powerful, and the poor and despised tremble not at the oppressor's frown. To such law every good citizen bows in cheerful submission, and with ready acquiescence, for it is but the embodied expression of his own sovereignty. But when, instead of the law of legislation, we have the law of the strongest, and, instead of judicial and executive administration, the summary inflictions of an infuriated mob, stung to madness by temporary rage, savage, remorseless and irresponsible, excited by some imagined insult or real injury, or perhaps by the expression of obnoxious and unpopular sentiments—we have a state of society at which the boldest may well tremble, and the most ardent despair.

*   *   *   *   *   *   *   *   *

"It is certainly a remarkable fact, that fifty-five years after the recognition of American independence by Great Britain, and the formal and precise demarkation of our limits, in the treaty of peace, the extent of those limits, and the territory rightfully subject to our jurisdiction, should be a matter of dispute and difference. I feel it to be my duty, in this my first official act, to call your attention to that vitally important question, the true limits of our State, and to express to you and the people my views of the claim set up by a foreign State to the rightful possession of a large part of our territory.

"I do not intend to enter into a historical detail, or an elaborate argument to sustain the American claim on our North Eastern Boundary. The whole subject has been for years before the people, and our rights, and the grounds upon which they rest, have been ably maintained, and clearly set forth, in our formal documents and informal discussions.

"I will not trespass needlessly upon your time and patience by a recapitulation. If there is any meaning in plain language, and any binding force in treaty engagements—if recognition and acquiescence for a long series of years on the part of Great Britain in one uniform expression and construction of the boundaries of her Provinces of Canada and Nova Scotia, is of any weight, then the right of Maine to the territory in dispute is as clear and unquestionable as to the spot upon which we now stand. It requires, indeed, the exercise of charity to reconcile the claim now made by Great Britain with her professions of strict integrity and high sense of justice in her dealings with other nations; for it is a claim of very recent origin, growing from an admitted right in us, and proceeding, first, to a request to vary our acknowledged line for an equivalent, and then, upon a denial, to a wavering doubt, and from thence to an absolute claim.

"It has required and still requires, all the talents of
her statesmen, and skill of her diplomatists, to render
that obscure and indefinite, which is clear and unam-
biguous.   I cannot for a moment doubt that if the same
question should arise in private life, in relation of the
boundaries of two adjacent farms, with the same evidence
and the same arguments, it would be decided by any
court, in any civilized country, without hesitation or
doubt, according to our claim.

"But Great Britain was anxious for a direct communication between her provinces.   She sought it first as a
favor and a grant.   She now demands about one third
part of our territory as her right.

"The pertinacity and apparent earnestness and confidence with which this claim is urged, in the very face of
the treaty, and the facts bearing upon the question,
have been increased, I fear, by the probably unexpected
forbearance, if not favor, with which they have been
received and treated by the American authorities.   It
can hardly be a matter of surprise that the claim is
pressed upon us, when instead of standing upon the
treaty—plain, definite and capable of execution as it
manifestly is—our own General Government has voluntarily suggested a variation of that line, certainly in
their favor, by running west of the due north line of the
treaty, and there to seek the highlands; thus yielding up
the starting point, the northwest angle of Nova Scotia,
and throwing the whole matter into uncertainty and confusion.   Fortunately for us, the English negotiators,
thinking, probably, that a nation which would yield
so much, would probably yield more, declined the
proposition, unless other concessions were made.   The
remarkable adjudication made by the arbiter selected
under the treaty, resulting merely in advice, the movement on the part of Maine, in 1832, in the negotiation

to yielding up the territory for an equivalent, the apparent apathy and indifference of the General Government to the encroaching jurisdiction by New Brunswick, her unopposed establishment of a wardenship over the territory—the repeated incarceration of the citizens of Maine, for acts done on this her territory, almost without a murmur of disapprobation or remonstrance, and the delay of the President to run the line as authorized by Congress, have all, I fear, served to strengthen and encourage the claim, which was first put forth with doubt and argued with many misgivings.

"The commission and arbitration under treaty having failed, and our ultra liberal offers either declined or neglected, the parties are turned back to their rights and their limits under the treaties of 1783 and 1814.

"But in truth, the only question in dispute, or about which there was any difference between the two governments, until since the last war and the last treaty, was to which river was the true St. Croix of the treaty. This being settled, and its head or source fixed, (as it has been) the line is to run due north to the south line of Canada, and the northwest angle of Nova Scotia. That line should be run without delay, as authorized by Congress.

"We warrant the information and the facts; we wish to examine the heighth of land which divides the waters flowing into the St. Lawrence from those running into the Atlantic, and ascertain its elevation and character. We wish to have our land marks placed on our exterior limits, and maintain our own.

"We wish to test the truth of the assertion, that there is no northwest angle of Nova Scotia, and no such dividing heighth of land as the treaty contemplates, by a correct and scientific examination on the face of the earth. Surely rights of examination, which are secured to individual claimants, are not to be denied to sovereign States.

"Our situation in relation to this question, owing to the peculiar nature of our government and institutions, is interesting, viewed either with reference to the foreign power with which we are at issue, or our own General Government. Our right and title, clear and perfect as we believe them to be, are, it must be admitted, subjects of dispute, and the first and great question is, how is this dispute to be settled? The line disputed is the Eastern boundary of the United States and of the State of Maine. The General Government is the only power which by the constitution can treat with a foreign government, or be acknowledged or known by that government, in negotiations. Maine acknowledges the right of the General Government to establish the line, according to the terms of the treaty of 1783, and claims a performance of that duty without delay. But whilst she concedes that power, she insists with equal confidence upon the position, that no variation of the treaty line, no concession of any part of our territory, and no conventional line can be granted or adopted, without the consent of this State.

"Whatever territory is included within the line running from the northwest angle of Nova Scotia westwardly along the highlands which divide those rivers that empty themselves into the St. Lawrence, from those which fall into the Atlantic ocean, to the northwesternmost head of the Connecticut river, and the line running directly south from said angle to the established source of the St. Croix, is within the State of Maine.

"If there is a dispute as to the location of that angle, and those lines—that question, and that question only, is to be settled by the general government.

"In making this assertion, we do not more distinctly acknowledge a power than claim the performance of a duty. In the first sentence of the Constitution of the United States, one of the important objects in the information of that constitution, as there expressed, is 'to provide for the common defence,' and this duty is afterwards in the same instrument, more specifically pointed out in the provision, that, 'The United States shall guarantee to every State in this Union a republican form of government, and shall protect each of them against invasion.' Under that constitution, the exercise of certain rights was denied to the States; all not expressly taken away were reserved to the States—and certain new rights were created.

"Foremost, and most important, of these newly created State rights, is the right, on the part of each State, to demand the aid of all, by the action of the general government, whenever any foreign power interferes with the territorial rights of such State.

"No State is to be left to defend its soil and maintain its just rights single handed and alone,—to engage in border skirmishes and partizan warfare, and sustain that warfare at its own expense.

"It is the duty of a State to claim and assert its rights to jurisdiction, and it is the duty of the general government to protect and maintain them, if just and well founded. The acknowledgement of this State right to protection is particularly important to Maine, environed by foreign territory, and forming a frontier State in the Union. Denied the power to negotiate with foreign governments, or to declare and carry on war in defence of her rights, this State can call, in a strong voice, upon that government to which has been delegated those high powers, for protection in the exercise of her jurisdictional rights. Perfect unity of purpose and frankness in disclosures ought to characterise all intercourse between the State and National Governments, on this topic. No course is so well calculated to lead to distrust and embarrassment, and to inspire confidence in the opposing claimants, as diplomatic evasions and jarring and discordant correspondence. We would use no threats of disunion or resistance. We trust that it will never be necessary for a State to assume a hostile attitude, or threatening language, to enforce practically its claims to protection.

"But Maine has a right to know, fully and explicitly, the opinion and determination of the general government, and whether she is to be protected, or left to struggle alone and unaided. I see little to hope from the forbearance or action of the British government. Their policy, it is apparent, is to delay a settlement of the question, and to extend their actual jurisdiction over the territory, that it may ripen into a right, or at least in future controversies give them the advantage of possession.

"The loose and extremely undefined jurisdiction over the small French Settlement at Madawaska, has been the foundation of a claim to actual jurisdiction, and the establishment of wardenship over the whole territory. In pursuance of this plan and policy, they have seized, at various times, heretofore, American citizens, and thrust them into prison, for alleged offences,—and during the past season, the Lieut. Governor of New Brunswick has visited the territory in person, and received the loyal assurance of such of its inhabitants as were ready to acknowledge their allegiance. A citizen of our State, Ebenezer S. Greeley, now lies imprisoned at Fredericton, seized, as it is said, for exercising power delegated to him under a law of this State. The facts connected with this arrest are unknown to me, and I therefore forbear to comment at this time upon them.

"If the facts are, that he was so seized, for such a lawful act, the dignity and sovereignty of the State and nation demand his immediate release.

"I am aware that we are met by the assertion that the parties have agreed to permit the actual jurisdiction to remain, pending the negotiation as it existed before. I have yet seen no evidence that such an agreement was ever formally entered into by the parties. But certainly Maine was no party to such an understanding, and at all events it could never have been intended to be perpetually binding, or to extend beyond the termination of the then pending negotiation. That negotiation is ended. The old ground of claim at Mars Hill is abandoned; a new allegation is made——that the treaty cannot be executed and must be laid aside. In the meantime this wardenship is established, and the claim to absolute jurisdiction, not merely at Madawaska, but over the whole territory north, is asserted and enforced.

"If this jurisdiction is to be tolerated and acquiesced in indefinitely, we can easily see why negotiation lags, and two years elapse between a proposition and the reply. They have all they want, and the jurisdiction is claimed by them so absolutely that we cannot send an agent to number the people, and must hesitate before the disputed line can be run, to fix our limits and ascertain important facts.

"The first duty of Maine, as it seems to me, is to claim the immediate action of the general government, to move efficiently and decidedly, to bring the controversy to a conclusion. We have had years of negotiation, and we are told that we are apparently no nearer to a termination than at the commencement. Maine has waited with most exemplary patience, until even her large stock is almost exhausted.

"She has no disposition to embarrass the action of the General Government, but she asks that some action be had—some movement made with a determined purpose to end the controversy.

"She cannot quietly submit to have her territory wrested from her, her citizens imprisoned, her territorial jurisdiction annihilated, and her rights lost by the bold and persevering and unopposed claims of a foreign power. She cannot consent to be left alone in the controversy, or to be left in doubt as to the aid or countenance she may receive from the authorities of the Union in maintaining her acknowledged rights. She asks the quiet and undisturbed possession of her territory, according to the treaty, and that foreign and intrusive possession be put an end to; and by this claim she will abide. She will do nothing rashly, and indulge in no spirit of nullification; and it will not be until all hope of settling the vexed question by negotiation, and all requests for other aid are denied or neglected, that she will throw herself entirely upon her own resources, and maintain, unaided and alone, her just rights, in the determined spirit of injured freemen. But those rights must be vindicated and maintained; and if all appeals for aid and protection are in vain, and her constitutional rights are disregarded, forbearance must cease to be a virtue—and, in the language of the lamented Lincoln, Maine may be 'compelled to deliberate on an alternative which will test the strictness of her principles and the firmness of her temper.' The recent movement in Congress by one of our Representatives—sustained, as we confidently trust, by his colleagues, gives some encouragement to hope that the day for decisive action is at hand.

"To you—delegated guardians of the people's rights

—I submit these remarks, and to you I leave the consideration of this momentous subject, confident that you will not yield to an unjust claim, or jeopardize our rights by delay in asserting them.   It is for you to say upon mature reflection, whether, in speaking in the name of Maine, I have exceeded the bounds of prudence, or mistaken the feelings of the people.   I confess that my convictions are strong, that Maine has been wronged by a foreign government, and neglected by our own— and I do not understand the diplomatic art of softening the expression of unpalatable truths.

"I can only assure you that I most cheerfully co-operate in maintaining our rights to protection in the exercise of our rightful jurisdiction."

From the time when the King of the Netherlands in 1831, rendered his decision until the whole matter came to a crisis in Maine in 1839, the Federal government did not make any decisive move that would be a notice to the world that her frontier in Maine was to be protected at all hazards.

History often repeats itself.   Then even more than now the party in power was inclined to consider first of all what effect such action would have upon its political fortunes.

President Jackson had not acted with his usual vigor and aggressiveness in any attempts to settle this question with England and preserve our rights, maintain our national honor, and protect the rights and honor of a sovereign state against the overt acts of a foreign power. He had disappointed his political friends and lent encouragement to his enemies in both Maine and Massachusetts.

President Van Buren took his seat in 1838, and, although the situation was much more serious than at any time during Jackson's administration, he was equally as inclined to procrastinate if not to vacillate about this subject of such vast importance, as was his predecessor.

During this period Maine had been ably represented in both houses of Congress.

In the Senate had been such men as Ether Shepley, Peleg Sprague, John Holmes and Reuel Williams.

In the lower house had been George Evans, F. O. J. Smith, Gorham Parks, Leonard Jarvis and Virgil D. Paris. It was at this time, 1837-39, that Thomas Davee of Blanchard was a representative.

The Maine delegation heartily supported by the Massachusetts delegation had been incessant in their efforts to force the administration to action.

Of their vigilance and faithfulness in this respect and their endeavors to constantly keep this issue a prominent one before the country there can be no doubt.

And yet eloquent speeches in Congress, convincing passages in Governors' messages and exciting reports and resolves of legislative committees, however much they might have aroused public sentiment in Maine, failed of having any salutory effect upon our arrogant neighbors across the border, sustained as they were by the powerful arm of Great Britain, so long as the policy of the national government was a passive one.

Rather did their magistrates become more defiant in claiming jurisdictional rights over the disputed territory, by issuing civil and criminal processes against the settlers along the Aroostook, Madawaska and upper St. John Rivers, and their officers more bold and domineering, and trespassing on these lands was increasing.

On the 14th of December, 1838, the land agents of Massachusetts and Maine, appointed George W. Buckmore an agent to proceed to the Fish Rivers, and investigate the trespassing by New Brunswick parties and prevent such trespassing if possible.

Based upon the report which Buckmore made to the land agent and other similar reports Governor Fairfield, January 23, 1839, submitted to the Legislature a message, in which he asserted that, "By this report it appears that a large number of men, many of them, I am informed, from the British provinces, are trespassing very extensively upon the lands belonging to this State: that, they not only refuse to desist, but defy the power of this government to prevent their cutting timber to any extent they please.

"Upon the Grand River, it is estimated there are from forty to fifty men at work. On the Green River, from twenty to thirty.

"On the Fish River, from fifty to seventy-five men with sixteen yoke of oxen and ten pair of horses, and more daily expected to go in. On township H ten men, six oxen and one pair of horses. On the little Madawaska seventy-five men, with twenty yoke of oxen and ten horses. At the Aroostook Falls fifteen men with six yoke of oxen.

"The quantity of timber which these trespassers will cut the present winter is estimated in value, by the Land Agent at one hundred thousand dollars."

And the Governor very pertinently remarked that it was not merely the property that was at stake, but "the character of the State is clearly involved."

He recommended to the Legislature that the land agent be instructed forthwith to proceed to the place of operation on the Aroostook and Fish Rivers with a sufficient number of men suitably equipped, to "seize the teams and provisions, break up the camps, and disperse those who are engaged in this work of devastation and pillage."

In this report Mr. Buckmore* says: "During my stop at the Madawaska settlement, I was called upon by Francis Rice, and Leonard R. Coombs, Esquires, two of the Magistrates living at Madawaska, to learn my business on the St. John River, which I freely communicated. They said they were authorized by the Governor to arrest all persons attempting to exercise jurisdiction, on the part of the American Government, in the Madawaska settlement, and that they should forward a copy of my instructions to the Governor at Fredericton."

January 24, 1839, the Legislature passed a resolve instructing and empowering the land agent to carry out the recommendations of the Governor and appropriating ten thousand dollars for the purpose.

In 1838, the Democrats had defeated Governor Kent, the Whig governor, and were again in power in Maine and had elected John Fairfield, governor, who was inaugurated in 1839.

He appointed Rufus McIntire of Parsonsfield, land agent.

Mr. McIntire was unquestionably a man of ability and integrity. He was a lawyer and had represented his district in Congress four terms.

Pursuant to the legislative resolve above referred to Governor Fairfield ordered the land agent to go to the Aroostook and Madawaska country for the purpose of carrying out the provisions of the resolve.

Mr. McIntire employed Major Hastings Strickland of Bangor, then sheriff of Penobscot County, to accompany and assist him in this work.

Consequently an expedition left Bangor during the first week of February, 1839, consisting of the land agent, Major Hastings Strickland, with a large civil

*Buckmore's report was made to Elijah L. Hamlin, land agent, in 1838.

RUFUS McINTIRE
LAND AGENT OF MAINE, 1839

posse, Ebenezer Webster and Captain Stover Rines of Orono, and Gustavus G. Cushman of Bangor.

They proceeded to the mouth of the Little Madawaska River, where they encamped.

During the night of February 12, the house or camp where McIntire slept was surrounded by about forty armed men. McIntire and those with him were awakened, placed under arrest and ordered to be ready at once to march to Fredericton. McIntire demanded by what authority they arrested him, and the commander pointing his musket at McIntire's breast, said, "This is our authority."

They were taken before a magistrate at Woodstock, who issued a warrant against Land Agent McIntire, Gustavus G. Cushman and Thomas B. Bartlett of Bangor, and they were forthwith marched to Fredericton and lodged in jail.

On Sunday, February 17th, the citizens of Bangor enjoyed the sight of two of the leading men among the province trespassers, Mr. McLaughlin, warden of the public lands in New Brunswick, and Captain Tibbets of the Tobique settlement, being escorted as prisoners through the streets of that city.

They had been captured by the Maine soldiers a few days before and were taken to Bangor, but unlike the prisoners captured by the British they were not lodged in the Bangor jail, but were lodged in the Bangor House and fared sumptuously.*

---

*The Bangor Whig, in speaking of this occurrence, editorially, remarked:

"It is worthy of remark and remembrance, that our Land Agent, when passing through Woodstock, was greeted with jeers and insults by British Subjects, but when the British Land Agent rode through this city, although there were over a thousand people assembled in the streets, he was suffered to pass in silence. Not a lip was opened or an insult offered."

On March 1, 1839, news was received in Bangor that a regiment of eight hundred Fusileers had arrived in the city of St. John, from Cork, Ireland, and would march forthwith to the disputed territory. Five hundred British Regulars had arrived at Madawaska from the city of Quebec, and eight pieces of cannon had been transported up the St. John River from Fredericton. The people of Maine were kept informed of the doings at the "Seat of War" by special messengers, stages and express teams, daily coming into Bangor. The Bangor Whig was published daily, and was one of the most enterprising of the Maine newspapers of the day.

It kept a "war correspondent" at Houlton and had a column or more in every issue for several weeks, giving graphic descriptions of the scenes of "war," of the hardships which were encountered, and of the soldiers tenting on the melting snow-drifts, all the way from Houlton to Madawaska. Some of this correspondence would have done credit to the "stories" of the "yellow" journals of today.

In one of these letters, published March 7th, the writer says: * * * * "let us give every hireling and subject of a monarchy, that grant to territory, which King Harold of yore was willing to give to the Norwegian King—seven feet by two."

The news of that day and the editorials in the papers at the time, were more or less colored by the issues of Maine politics. The Bangor Whig was violently partisan and for a time did not give Governor Fairfield, who was a Democrat, and had been chosen governor over Governor Kent, credit for being either competent or patriotic. But as the public mind became intensified in favor of protecting our border, it changed its course and was soon supporting his official acts as loyally as did

The Argus, The Age, or any of the Democratic papers.

When Sheriff Strickland first went to the Aroostook with his posse, and when McIntire was taken prisoner by Sir John Harvey's officers, the Whig papers contended that McIntire* left his camp and troops and went within a mile of the enemy to obtain a feather bed to sleep upon, and was thus seen and captured, and that if he had been content to have reposed upon spruce boughs he would not have fallen into the toils of the enemy.

Some slurs were also cast upon Hastings Strickland for what they termed his "untimely haste," in escaping from the British officers, intimating that he was cowardly, and retreated very unceremoniously. The facts however were that he was alert enough not to be taken prisoner, as some of his companions were, and perceived at once the necessity for immediate and decisive action on the part of Governor Fairfield and Adjutant General Hodgdon, if Maine's rights were to be protected. Being a man of great energy he went from Madawaska to Augusta as rapidly as relays of swift horses would carry him† for the purpose of prevailing upon the State government at Augusta to mobilize troops upon the border without further delay. Major Strickland was a man of political sagacity and a leader of influence in the Democratic party, and one that Governor Fairfield relied upon for advice and counsel.

Naturally both political parties tried to make political capital for themselves; the effect of which was to hinder efficient progress in protecting our frontier.

The Democrats criticized Governor Kent in 1838, and

---

*When McIntire was imprisoned Governor Fairfield appointed Colonel Charles Jarvis provisional land agent.

†Bangor newspapers stated that Major Strickland did not even stop at his home in Bangor but proceeded directly to Augusta.

in turn the Whigs blamed Governor Fairfield whenever it was possible to do so.

As the "Aroostook War" or the military movement of troops to the frontier was made under Governor Fairfield, the Whigs for many years thereafter, kept up an incessant fire of ridicule against him, and Land Agent McIntire and Major Strickland.

In this way it became a false tradition that the latter ran away from a conflict to escape imprisonment. One of the doggerels of the day commenced:

> "Run, Strickland, run!
> Fire, Stover, fire!
> Were the last words of McIntire."

In the meantime the situation was becoming more and more inflammatory. It was the subject of discussion and agitation in England as well as America. On the 7th of March, 1839, both Lord Brougham and the Duke of Wellington made speeches regarding it in the House of Lords, calling attention to information which had been received from Canada and New Brunswick to the effect that lawless Yankees were invading and trespassing upon the British soil.

When the people of Maine received news of the proclamation of Sir John Harvey, lieutenant-governor of New Brunswick, of February 13, 1839, which was a declaration of war, and the imprisonment of the land agent, the feeling of indignation was deep and universal.

The Legislature appropriated eight hundred thousand dollars to be used by the Governor for the protection of the public lands.

A draft was also ordered for ten thousand three hundred and forty-three men from the militia to be ready for immediate action.

General Bachelder was commander of the western division of militia. Many volunteers from Penobscot and Piscataquis Counties and other eastern portions of the State were also enlisted.

Within a week ten thousand American troops were either in the Aroostook region, or on the march there.

The national government was at last awake to the seriousness of the situation. Congress passed a bill authorizing the President of the United States to raise fifty thousand troops for the support of Maine, and appropriating ten million dollars to meet the expense if war became unavoidable.

General Scott was ordered to the scene of action, informing Governor Fairfield that he was "specially charged with maintaining the peace and safety of the entire northern and eastern frontiers." He arrived in Augusta with his staff the fifth of March, 1839, and opened headquarters.

General Scott was also clothed with full power to act as mediator between the State of Maine and the Province of New Brunswick, and on entering upon negotiations which would if possible end further hostilities. He immediately communicated officially with Governor Fairfield and Sir John Harvey.

The result was that on March 23, 1839, Sir John Harvey agreed to the terms of settlement negotiated by General Scott, and on March 25 the same were ratified by Governor Fairfield, who immediately issued orders to recall the troops from the Aroostook and the prisoners on both sides were liberated.

Thus ended the famous "Aroostook War," and fortunately for the people of the State and the province it was a bloodless one. It has been derided and scoffed at and regarded as a huge international joke, and often has it been the subject for jest and laughter on the stump, and ever a fertile field for the grotesque wit of newspaper writers.

And yet it is an incident in international history, in the history of the nation, and of the State of Maine, that is of supreme importance and interest.

For years its solution puzzled the wisest of our statesmen. The people of Maine believed that the territory which they possessed, and to which no one else had any rightful or lawful interest, was being wrongfully and illegally taken from them and that the government at Washington delayed the assertion of our rights unnecessarily, because it feared Great Britain.

Two expeditions were made to the Aroostook and Madawaska country. The first one as we have seen, was by the land agent, accompanied by Major Strickland as sheriff of Penobscot County, with a posse of men, for the purpose of driving off trespassers upon Maine soil. The second expedition was a military one to repel an invasion of the State, which the lieutenant-governor of New Brunswick, Sir John Harvey, had threatened to make.

Patriotic sons of the Pine Tree State left their homes and firesides in the most inclement season known to our rigorous climate and marched through the deep snows of a wilderness, two hundred miles, to defend our frontier from foreign invasion, when the Federal government was needlessly procrastinating and turning a deaf ear to the cries of suffering and oppressed pioneers in the upper St. John valley.

Because the good fortunes of diplomacy triumphed and averted the shedding of blood, is no reason why they are not entitled to a high place in the roll of honor, with all of the other hosts of patriotic defenders of our country, and the protection of her glory and renown.

In his annual message January 3, 1840, Governor Fairfield in referring to the Resolves of the Legislature, passed in March, 1839, explains the withdrawal of the troops, by saying: "Soon after the adoption of the resolution, I received the written assent of the Lieutenant Governor of New Brunswick to the following, made to him by Major General Scott, to wit: 'That it is not the intention of the Lieutenant Governor of Her Britannic Majesty's Province of New Brunswick, under the expected renewal of negotiations between the Cabinets of London and Washington on the subject of said disputed territory, without renewed instructions to that effect, from his government, to seek to take military possession of that territory, or to seek by military force, to expel the armed civil posse or the troops of Maine.' "

Upon the basis of this arrangement the troops were recalled by the Governor, but he kept quite a large force or civil posse there after the withdrawal of the troops, under the direction and control of the land agent.

But war between the United States and England was averted through friendly diplomacy. What is known as the Webster-Ashburton treaty in American history was its final adjustment. This treaty was negotiated by Daniel Webster and Lord Alexander Baring Ashburton in August, 1842, and subsequently accepted and ratified by both governments.

The commissioners who represented the State of Maine at the hearings before Webster and Ashburton were Edward Kavanagh, Edward Kent, Wm. P. Preble and John Otis.

On the part of Massachusetts appeared Abbot Lawrence, John Mills and Charles Allen.

At this treaty the frontier line between the State of Maine and Canada was settled for all time.

By it, seven twelfths of the disputed ground, including that part of Madawaska that lies on the southerly side of the St. John River, were given to the United States, and five twelfths of the ground to Great Britain; but it secured a better military frontier for England, and included heights commanding the St. Lawrence, which the award of the King of the Netherlands had assigned to the Americans.

MAJOR HASTINGS STRICKLAND
SHERIFF OF PENOBSCOT COUNTY, 1838-9

DOCUMENTARY HISTORY OF THE NORTH EASTERN BOUNDARY CONTROVERSY

Documentary History of the North Eastern Boundary Controversy

(From State Papers, 2nd Sess. 20th Cong. 1828-9, Doc. No. 90.)

Report of the trial of John Baker, at the Bar of the Supreme Court, on Thursday, the 8th May, 1828, for conspiracy.

In the Hilary term of the Supreme Court, the Grand Jury for the county of York found a true bill of indictment against John Baker, James Bacon and Charles Studson, for conspiracy. The two defendants, James Bacon and Charles Studson, were not taken; but the defendant, John Baker, being in custody, was brought to the bar and arraigned, and thereupon pleaded not guilty, at the same time protesting against the proceedings, and that he was not amenable to the jurisdiction of this court.

He was afterwards, during the term, admitted to bail, and entered into recognizance, himself in £100, and two sureties in £50 each, for his appearance at the present term, to traverse the indictment, and in the meantime to keep the peace and be of good behavior.

On Wednesday, the 7th instant, the Attorney General states to the Court, that, having understood the defendant, John Baker, was in attendance, he should be ready, at the opening of the Court on the next day, to proceed with the trial. One of the bail for the defendant then said that the defendant would appear whenever he was required. Thursday was, therefore, appointed by the Court for the trial.

Thursday, May 8, 1828.

The honorable Chief Justice Saunders,
Mr. Justice Bliss,
Mr. Justice Chipman,
came into court, and took their seats.

The defendant, John Baker, was called, and appeared, and declared he was ready for his trial: Mr. Attorney General then moved for trial, and the clerk of the crown proceeded to call over the names of the jury.

Mr. Justice Chipman stated to the defendant that he might challenge any of the jurors for cause, but he declined availing himself of this privilege.

The following jurors were called, and sworn in the order they appeared:

Michael Fisher,	Joseph Estabrooks, Jr.,
William Miller,	John Collins,
Edward Cambridge,	Samuel Curry,
John Bain,	Thomas W. Peters,
Joseph Sutherland,	William S. Esty,
Donald McLeod,	Anthony Stewart.

The clerk of the crown then read the indictment, which is as follows:

York, to wit. The jurors for our lord the King, upon their oath, present, that John Baker, late of the parish of Kent, in the county of York, laborer, James Bacon, late of the same place, laborer, and Charles Studson, late of the same place, laborer, being persons greatly disaffected to our said lord the now King, and his government, within this, His Majesty's Province of New Brunswick, and being factiously and seditiously disposed, on the fourth day of July, in the eighth year of the reign of our said sovereign lord George the

Fourth, with force and arms, at the parish aforesaid, in the county aforesaid, did, amongst themselves, conspire, combine, confederate, and agree together, falsely, maliciously, factiously, and seditiously, to molest and disturb the peace and common tranquility of this Province, and to bring into hatred and contempt our said lord the King, and his Government, and to create false opinions and suspicions in the subjects of our said lord the King, of and concerning the Government and administration of our said lord the King, and of the royal power and prerogative of our said lord the King within this Province.

First overt act. And the jurors aforesaid, upon their oath aforesaid, do further present, that the said John Baker, James Bacon, and Charles Studson, afterwards, to wit, on the same day and year aforesaid, at the parish aforesaid, in the county aforesaid, in pursuance of, and according to, the said conspiracy, combination, confederacy and agreement, amongst themselves had as aforesaid, did erect, and cause to be raised and erected, a certain flag staff, and did place thereon a certain flag, as the standard of the United States of America, and did then and there declare, in the presence and hearing of divers liege subjects of our said lord the King, that the said place on which the same flag staff was so erected was a part of the territory of the said United States, and that they, the said liege subjects, must thereafter, look upon themselves as subjects of the said United States.

Second overt act. And the jurors aforesaid, upon their oath aforesaid, do further present, that the said John Baker, James Bacon, and Charles Studson, afterwards, to wit, on the 15th day of July aforesaid, in the year aforesaid, at the parish aforesaid, in the county aforesaid, in further pursuance of, and according to, the said conspiracy, combination, confederacy and agreement, amongst themselves had as aforesaid, applied to divers liege subjects of our said lord the King, and then and there presented to the same subjects a paper writing, which they, the said John Baker, James Bacon, and Charles Studson, then and there requested the said subjects to sign, then and there declaring that, by the said paper, they, the said subjects would bind themselves to oppose the execution of the laws of Great Britain, to wit, in the Madawaska settlement, so called.

Third overt act. And the jurors, aforesaid, upon their oath aforesaid, do further present, that the said John Baker, James Bacon, and Charles Studson, afterwards, to wit, on the 18th day of July, in the year aforesaid, in further pursuance of, and according to, the said conspiracy, combination, confederacy and agreement, amongst themselves had as aforesaid, did oppose and obstruct the postman then and there having the custody and carriage of His Majesty's mail to the Province of Lower Canada, in the prosecution of his journey with the said mail; they, the said John Baker, James Bacon, and Charles Studson, declaring to the said postman that the British Government had no right to send its mails by that route, meaning through that part of the said parish of Kent called the Madawaska settlement; and that they, the said John Baker, James Bacon, and Charles Studson, had received orders from the Government of the said United States to stop the carriage of the said mail through the same.

Fourth overt act. And the jurors aforesaid, upon their oath aforesaid, do further present, that the said John Baker, James Bacon, and Charles Studson, afterwards, to wit, on the tenth day of August, in the year aforesaid, at the parish aforesaid, in the county aforesaid, in further pursuance of, and according to, the said conspiracy, combination, confederacy, and agreement, amongst themselves had as aforesaid, did hoist the flag of the said United States of America on a certain flag staff there erected and placed; they, the said John Baker, James Bacon, and Charles Studson, then and there declaring, in the presence and hearing of divers subjects of our said lord the King, that they, the said John Baker, James Bacon, and Charles Studson, had so hoisted the same flag, and that they had mutually entered into a written agreement to keep the same flag there, and that nothing but a force superior to their own should take it down; and further, that they considered, and had a right to consider, themselves then and there on the territory of the said United States; and that they had bound themselves to resist by force the execution of the laws of Great Britain among them there; in very great contempt of our said lord the King and his laws, to the evil example of all others in the like case offending, and against the peace of our said lord the King, his crown and dignity.

The Attorney General, who conducted the prosecution, then opened the case to the jury, and stated generally the nature of the offence, and the facts necessary to be proved in order to support the indictment: he then briefly set forth the evidence which he intended to adduce to substantiate the charge; and particularly stated it would be shown that the jurisdiction of this Province had always extended over the part of this country where the offence was committed: that the defendants were acting under no authority whatever; and this was an indictment found by the grand jury in the ordinary exercise of their duties. He desired the jury to dismiss from their mind every thing that they had heard or seen written on this case, and decide on the guilt or innocence of the party by the evidence alone; and, if they could

not conscientiously say he was guilty, to acquit him.
Several authorities were then read; but as the whole case
was most fully and ably gone into by the learned judge
who charged the jury, and the same view of the law and
facts taken by him as by the Attorney General, it is not
necessary to go into a full detail of the opening speech.

Mr. Attorney General then proceeded to call the witnesses.

William Feirio, one of the witnesses recognized at
the last term, was called but did not appear.

George Morehouse was the first witness examined:
his evidence was as follows:

I am a Justice of the Peace for the county of York,
and reside in the parish of Kent, on the river St. John,
about thirty miles below the Grand Falls. The Madawaska settlers commence a few miles above the Falls,
and extend up forty to fifty miles. I have been settled
where I now live six years; but my acquaintance with
the Madawaska settlement commenced in the year 1819.
At this time the inhabitants were principally French;
there were a few American citizens. I cannot say
whether defendant was there then; his brother Nathan
was. I do not recollect the defendant's being there
until September, 1822: he and the other Americans had
formed a lumbering establishment at the head of the
Madawaska settlement, on the east side of the river St.
John, by the Meriumpticook stream. That part of the
country where the French and Americans were has been
invariably under the jurisdiction and laws of this Province
since I knew it. I have been in the constant habit, as
a Magistrate, of sending my writs and warrants there,
and no interruption or objection was made to the service
of them until last August, until then, it was my belief
that all the inhabitants there considered themselves
under the jurisdiction of, and subject to, the laws of

this Province, both American citizens and French settlers.

When I speak of last August, I mean that this was
the first intimation I had of any objection being made
to the exercise of the jurisdiction of this Province there.
That intimation was made by a report or communication
from Mr. Rice, that John Baker, the defendant, had
been guilty of seditious practices. I forwarded the
communication to the Secretary of the Province; a few
days after, about the third of August, I received written instructions from His Majesty's Attorney General to
proceed to Madawaska and take depositions, and get a
copy of the written paper which it was reported the
defendants had handed about for signature. I accordingly proceeded to Madawaska on the seventh of August,
and arrived at the place where Baker's house is situate,
and went into the house of James Bacon, and asked him
to let me see the paper which had been handed about for
signature: he said he had it not. I then requested
Bacon to go with me to Baker's to look for the paper;
he declined going: I then went towards Baker's house,
and met him on his mill dam. The mill dam is made
across the river Meriumpticook. I stated to him that
it had been reported to Government that he and other
American citizens residing there had been guilty of
seditious practices; that I was authorized to make
inquiry. I told him it was reported that he had drawn
up, and circulated among the settlers, a paper, the
purport of which was that they were American citizens,
and had bound themselves to resist the execution of the
laws of Great Britain: he neither admitted or denied it,
but said that he had been charged with an attempt to
stop the mail, which was false. I requested him to show
me the paper which had been handed round for signature: he said he believed it was not in his possession,

but did not deny the existence of such a paper: he said he did not know whether it was in his possession or not; he thought Studson had it. I requested him to go to his house and search his papers; perhaps he might find it; we proceeded together towards his house; between his residence and the mill, there is a new house, where ten or twelve Americans were assembled. I did not know them to be Americans: but supposed them to be so; they were not French settlers: when we got there, Baker took two or three aside, and consulted with them a few minutes; he then came back, and said to me, "Mr. Morehouse, I have consulted with the committee, and we have determined that you shall not see this paper: we have formerly shown you papers in similar cases, which has been very prejudicial to us." I observed, when I went there, a flag staff erected on the point of land where Baker lives; the point is formed by the junction of the Meriumpticook river with the St. John; there was then no flag on it, but after coming out of Bacon's, I observed a flag hoisted—a white flag, with an American eagle and semicircle of stars, red. In the conversation I had with Bacon he deprecated Baker's practices, and said he would not desist until he brought the Americans there into trouble. I think the persons Baker took aside to consult with, were Bartlett and Savage. After I had received the answer before mentioned, I pointed to the flag, and asked Baker what that was. He said, "the American flag, Mr. Morehouse: did you never see it before, if not, you can see it now." I asked him who planted it there: he said, "he and the other Americans there." Bacon was present at the time: I required him in His Majesty's name to pull it down. He replied, "no, I will not; we have placed it there, and we are determined we will support it, and nothing but a superior force to ourselves shall take it down; we are on American territory; Great Britain has no jurisdiction here; what we are doing we will be supported in; we have a right to be protected, and will be protected, in what we are doing, by our Government."

He did not produce or exhibit any authority. I then turned to Bacon, and said, "Bacon, you have heard Baker's declaration, do you mean to support him in it?" He said, "of course I do." I then left him and came away. Baker, about the 1st February, 1825, applied to me, as a Magistrate, for summonses against some of the Madawaska settlers to collect debts. I gave him six summonses against persons all living in the Madawaska settlement: the return made to me was that the debts were paid when the writs were served.

Baker has a considerable improvement, and raises more or less grain every year. In 1823, I was at the place where he resides. I understood from what passed, that Baker and Bacon both acknowledged they had signed the paper; they spoke of having bound themselves by a written agreement to resist the laws of England.

The direct examination having closed, the defendant was informed he might cross-question the witness: he declined doing it, saying, under the circumstances which he stood there, he did not intend asking any questions.

To questions then put by the Court, the witness stated:

The Madawaska settlement proper terminates at the Madawaska river; above the river, there are a few miles interval, with a few scattering houses; the main settlement then commences about nine miles above the Madawaska, and extends seven or eight miles. The Meriumpticook is about eighteen miles above the Madawaska. This settlement has formerly gone by the name of Chateaugay: Lately it has been called Sainte Emilie by the

French settlers in the settlement. I mean distinctly that the upper as well as the lower settlement has been subject to the British laws. It is at the head of the settlement the Americans reside. The whole settlement has gone by the general name of Madawaska Settlement throughout the country; the name Chateaugay caused some difference amongst themselves; the Priest changed it to Sainte Emilie; there has been no distinction in the actual exercise of jurisdiction between the upper and lower part of this settlement; the lower bound of the parish of Kent is eighteen miles below my residence.

Francis Rice sworn. I reside in the Madawaska settlement, at the head or the first part. I am adjutant of the fourth battalion York county militia: the Madawaska settlers are enrolled in this battalion. I have been in court, and heard Mr. Morehouse's evidence. I made a report to him, as he has stated. I did not know the facts myself; they were reported to me. I accompanied Mr. Morehouse on his visit to the settlement on the 7th August last, and was present at the conversations with Baker and Bacon: the facts all took place as he has stated: I can say nothing more. The Madawaska settlers attend and turn out at the militia training pretty regularly, both above and below the confluence of the Madawaska.

The French settlers not being able to speak English distinctly, the witness, Francis Rice, had previously been sworn as interpreter, and acted as such throughout the trial.

Abraham Chamberlain sworn. I live in the upper part of the Madawaska settlement, above the Madawaska river; have resided there four years this Summer; was born at Bay Chaleur; came from there to this Province four years ago and have always lived since in the Madawaska settlement. Charles Studson presented me a paper, I think in July last. I don't remember seeing Baker. Bacon and Emery, and some other Americans, were present. I was passing by; they were drinking rum; they asked me to take some; I agreed. When they handed the paper, I asked whether any of the French had signed it; they said, not yet.

The witness being then asked as to the contents of the paper, and the propriety of such evidence being questioned by the court, the Attorney General cited the case of Rex versus Hunt and others, 3 Barn. and Ald. 566, where it was decided, on an indictment for conspiracy, that secondary evidence of the contents of a paper which was in the defendant's possession was admissible without producing the original, or giving notice to produce it; and that parole evidence of inscriptions and devices on banners and flags is also admissible. The question was then put; but the witness could say nothing as to the contents, stating that it was read to him, but, being in English, he did not understand it. They asked him to sign it; but he did not understand for what reason. He wanted to know whether any of the French had signed it. This took place at the point of land near the mill. There was a flag hoisted with an eagle and stars on it; they did not say anything about having signed the paper themselves.

Peter Marque sworn. I live in the St. Emilie settlement, (the upper one.) Bacon and Studson, some time last Summer, tried to make me sign a paper. Studson handed it to me; I do not know for what reason: they read the paper, but I did not understand it, and asked whether the French had signed it: they said, not yet. I then said I would not sign it. I told Mr. Morehouse they wanted me to sign a paper. This was at the place where the pole stands. I never understood the purpose for which I was called to sign the paper. I worked

.eleven days for Baker last year, at the time of getting
hay : I now work for myself. They told me Chamberlain had signed the paper. I dont remember anything
more.

Peter Sileste sworn. I was employed last Summer to
carry the mail from Madawaska to Lake Timisconatee :
as I was taking it up the river, polling up in a canoe, I
met John Baker coming down the river on a raft; he
came off to me in a small skiff; neither of us stopped.
Baker asked me in English, "Do you carry the mail?"
I said "Yes." He said he had orders from America
not to let the mail pass that way. I replied, I had no
orders to stop there. This was all that passed. This
was, I think, in July.

Joseph Sanfason sworn. I live in the Madawaska
settlement, half a mile below the Green river : the Green
river is below the Madawaska. I was born at Madawaska. I bought land from J. Souci : he had a grant
from the government of this Province. I bought it
six years ago. I have been a constable for two years
for the parish of Kent. I was obstructed in my duty
of constable by Baker, Bacon, Bartlett, Savage, Shelly,
and Jones. I had an execution from Mr. Morehouse
against J. Bacon. I asked Bacon if he would come?
He said he would not leave the place. Baker said, it
is of no use for you to go there; you shall not have
the man. Bacon talked about settling it. Baker said,
Bacon you must not settle it now; you must settle it
another time; I will not allow any officer to go up
there. He asked me if I had any authority to go
there. I showed him the warrant: he said, if it came
from the States he would mind it; but it was only from
Mr. Morehouse, and he would not mind it. They prevented my taking Bacon, who refused to go. This
took place near Baker's mill.

Edward William Miller, Esq., sworn. I am high sheriff of the county of York, and have been so since 1814. I have been acquainted with the Madawaska settlement seven years. I never could make any division in the settlement between the upper and the lower. When I first knew it, it extended to seven miles from the Falls; lately, it has come within three or four miles. I know the Meriumpticook river. I have been in the habit of serving writs throughout the whole of the settlement, the same as in any other part of my baili-wick. When I first became acquainted with the settle-ment, I considered the inhabitants under the jurisdic-tion and government of this Province, without any dis-pute whatever. The distance is so great, I have never summoned them as jurors: it would be so inconvenient to attend: the inhabitants serve in the militia. I never met with any obstruction in the discharge of my duty.

Peter Fraser, Esq., sworn. I have been an inhabit-ant of this Province since 1784: am acquainted with the Madawaska settlement. It is about seven or eight years since I was first there; but I have been acquainted with the settlers since 1787. I considered them always under the government of this Province. The first settler I knew was Capt. Duperree, a captain of the militia of this Province: the date of his commission was between 1787 and 1790. He resided in the settlement. The settlers have voted at elections: there was some difficulty at first in their doing so, on account of the oath which was required to be taken, as they were Catholics; but when this was altered, they have voted without diffi-culty. To my own knowledge, they voted in 1809, and ever since. I consider the Madawaska settlement as extending from the Great Falls to the Canada line. I have been where Baker lives; and always deemed the part above the Madawaska river as in the Madawaska settlement. There is no distinction, in this respect, between what is above and below that river. The Madawaska settlers are enrolled in the militia of this Province; in Captain Duperree's time, there were two companies. In 1824, they were formed into a separate battalion, consisting of five companies: I am major of the battalion. They turn out very regularly. I never heard of their making any objections to training.

Henry Clopper sworn. I am clerk of the peace and register of deeds for this county. I was appointed clerk in 1823, and register in 1821. I succeeded my father in both offices. I have discharged the duties since 1820, having acted for him before receiving the appointment myself. Parish officers were appointed by the sessions for the parish of Kent. There was a separate list for the Madawaska district, in that parish. I have been as far up the river as ten miles above the Grand Falls. There are a great many deeds registered in my office of land in Madawaska, where the parties are the Madawaska settlers, some as long since as twenty-five or thirty years back. As clerk of the peace, I receive the money given as bounty for grain raised on new ground in this county. In May, 1825, the defendant, John Baker, applied to me for the bounty for grain raised by him on new land. He received the bounty from me. The paper now produced by me is the document under which he became entitled to it. I observed to him that he was an alien, and I was not aware whether he was strictly entitled to it. He said his certificate had passed the session. The paper I now hold is the certificate, and the only one; it has been on file in my office since.

The paper was here put in, and read by the clerk of the Crown, and is as follows:

"I, John Baker, of Kent, do swear that ninety

bushels of wheat were really and truly raised on the land occupied by me, and are actually of the crop of the year 1823, (1822) and that the wood was cut down, burnt, or cleared off from the land on which the same was raised within two years previous to the time that the said crop was taken off, and that they were of the first and only crop of grain raised on land from which the said wood was so cut down, burnt, or cleared off, as aforesaid.

"John Baker.

"Sworn before me, at Woodstock, the 2d of July, 1825, (1823.)

"John Bedell, Justice of the Peace.

"I verily believe the facts above stated to be just and true.

"John Bedell."

I paid him by a check on Mr. Needham; the amount was £4 5s 3d; this is the order I gave Mr. Needham.

Cross-examined by defendant. Have you got the receipt I gave for the money? The witness here produced the schedule and signature to it by Baker, and said this is the only receipt he gave me, except the one given to Mr. Needham.

Mark Needham sworn. I remember the circumstance of paying this order; the words "received payment" on it are in my writing. I have no doubt I paid it, but have not now any particular recollection of the defendant. I considered it paid, and charged Mr. Clopper with it.

George I. Dibblee sworn. I am acquainted with the hand-writing of the defendant, John Baker—have seen him write; the signature to the receipt on the order is his hand-writing; I have no doubt of it.

Simon Abear, or Hibert, sworn. I live two miles below Madawaska river; have lived there four (forty) years next month; I moved there from the French vil-

lage about ten miles above Frederickton. I have a grant
of my land from this Province; it is the first grant in
the Madawaska, and was made about two or three years
after I moved up. I live under this government, and
have always lived under it; all the Madawaska settlers
live under the same Government. I vote at elections;
the first time was about eight years ago. Baker came
last year to my house; he asked me what time I go to
train my company; I am a captain of militia; he said
there is not much occasion to train at Madawaska. I
inquired the reason; he said nothing; I told him I
would go next Saturday—he must be stronger than me
to prevent me. I know where Baker lives; he came five
or six years ago; he has always lived at the same place—
raised grain there; I believe he cultivated no where else.
Baker said I had better not train but did (not) ask me
not to train.

George West sworn. I know the defendant, Baker;
have known him since 1820; he was then settled at the
Bay Chaleur; I saw him next at the Madawaska; this
was when Judge Bliss was President, I believe 1824. I
seized 300 logs from him; I was then a seizing officer;
he said he wished to become a British subject, as he had
been here the necessary time; he inquired of me what
steps it would be necessary for him to take; I told him
as far as my information went; this was at the place
where he lives; it is called Baker's mill stream; he spoke
as if he considered himself a resident within this Province, and wished to have all the lenity shown him on
that account; it was shown him; he was allowed to
redeem the loss at the rate of 2s 6d per thousand feet,
counting three logs to a thousand. The logs were seized
as cut on Crown lands without license. I have seen him
since; there was a warrant of survey sent to me to execute
of this land where Baker resides; it was in Samuel

Nevers' name; Baker himself attended the execution of the warrant, and directed the course of the lines; the privilege was considered Baker's, but taken in Nevers' name, as Baker was not a British subject: I think this was about two years ago.

The evidence on the part of the prosecution having here closed, the defendant was called upon for his defence; he addressed the court nearly as follows:

"I am a citizen of the United States, and owe allegiance to that country. I have lately received my deed from the States of Maine and Massachusetts. I hold myself bound to their Courts. I live in American territory, and hold myself only liable to the courts of that place, being the county of Penobscot, in the State of Maine. I enter no defence, and call no evidence. I do decline the jurisdiction of this court."

The defendant alluded to a letter he had, in the course of the trial, handed to the Chief Justice; which was delivered to him, and he was informed he might, if he chose, read it as part of his defense, but declined doing so.

The Attorney General then addressed the Court, and said, that, as he had, in his opening, stated generally the nature of the case and evidence, and the defendant had not made any defence, he did not think it necessary, after so much time had been taken up and the evidence so fully gone into, to address the jury, but would merely read two or three additional authorities, (which he did, from Starkie's Evidence, Compyn's Digest, Blackstone's Commentaries, and Archbold's Criminal Pleading,) and then leave the case in the hands of the Court.

Mr. Justice Chipman charged the Jury. He began by stating the indictment and plea, the general nature of the offence, and the proofs requisite to support the charge. He said that the body of the offence was the conspiracy, and combining and confederating together with the intent laid in the indictment. In the present case, the intent charged was to bring into contempt the King's authority, to spread false opinions among his subjects as to his power and prerogative over them, and in fact completely to unsettle their minds as to their allegiance to the Government under which they lived. This mind and intention must be made manifest by overt acts. It was usual, though held not to be absolutely necessary, to set forth overt acts in the indictment; but if, from the facts proved in evidence, the jury should be satisfied that the defendant, Baker, now on trial, did combine and confederate with one or both of the other defendants named in the indictment with the intent imputed to them, that would be sufficient to make up the offence. As the essence of the crime was the combining, two persons at least must be engaged in it. The Judge then stated that before going into a consideration of the evidence, he would dispose of the ground which the defendant had set up when called upon his defence: which was, that the place where the acts were committed was in the territory of the United States, and that he, the defendant, was not amenable to the laws, or subject to the jurisdiction of the Courts of this Province. The Judge then stated that the question as to the national rights to this territory, now well known to be in controversy, is one which this Court is utterly incompetent to enter into, and can have nothing to do with. It is a matter of state, to be settled between the two nations, Great Britain and the United States; to be dealt with by the Governments of the two countries, and not by this Court. The Court will only inquire whether the place in question is actually in the possession and under the jurisdiction, and laws of this Province; and if so, the Court will maintain that jurisdiction, and continue the exercise and protection of those laws, until some act of the King's Government shall effect a change. There can be no stronger evidence of the possession of a country than the free and uncontrolled exercise of jurisdiction within it; and the Court is bound by its allegiance to the Crown, and its duty to the King's subjects, to act upon this, which it considers as the only principle truly applicable to the case. This principle has already been acted upon in this Province.

The learned Judge then referred to the case of the sloop Falmouth, adjudged in the Court of Vice Admiralty of this Province many years ago, (1806.) He stated this to have been the case of a seizure by a British officer of an American vessel lying in the waters of Passamaquoddy Bay, for landing her cargo within this Province; no foreign vessels being at that time admissible into the ports of these colonies. The counsel for the prosecution in that case went at large into the question of right to all the islands in that bay, under the provisions of the treaty of 1783, and contended that, by virtue of that treaty, all the islands, including Moose, Dudley, and Frederick Islands, then in the actual possession of the United States, of right belonged to Great Britain; and that no foreign vessel could lawfully lade (land) a cargo in any part of that bay; but the learned judge of that Court at that time, now one of the Judges of this Court, (Mr. Justice Botsford,) in pronouncing judgment, would not enter upon the question of right to the islands, which he considered a matter of state for the two Governments to decide upon; but finding the three islands beforenamed to be under the actual possession and jurisdiction of the United States, he applied the principle of the law of nations applicable to a water boundary between two different countries, and directed

his attention solely to the point whether the vessel
laded her cargo on the British side of a middle line drawn
between these islands then in the possession of the
United States, and the British islands opposite. It
thus appears that this doctrine of taking the actual
state of things as we find them, and applying the law
accordingly, has been already acted upon in this Province, in an instance where it was favorable to citizens
of the United States; and this Court has no hesitation
in applying the same doctrine, which it considers as
the true doctrine, to the present case. It is to be
observed that the defendant in the present case has
given no evidence whatever of the place in question
being in the possession or under the jurisdiction of
the United States; that he does not appear to be in
any respect an agent of that Government, or acting
under its authority; and that what has been done must
be considered as being altogether the acts of unauthorized individuals. The place where the transaction
occurred goes by the general name of the Madawaska
settlement; and if this settlement shall appear to be,
in point of fact, under the jurisdiction of this Province,
the case must receive the same consideration, and the
conduct of the defendant be viewed in the same light, as
if the acts complained of had been committed in any
other part of the Province, one hundred miles further
down on the river St. John, or even in this town of
Frederickton.

The learned Judge then proceeded to read over the
whole of the testimony from his notes, commenting upon
the several parts of it as he went on. He considered the
overt acts as to hoisting of the flag of the United
States with the express intention of subverting British
authority, as most distinctly and fully proved and asked
what more unequivocal indication there could be of an

intention to bring the King's Government into contempt, and of unsettling the administration of the laws of the Province, than the erecting of a foreign standard with this declared purpose. With respect to the transaction with the postman he directed the jury that if they considered the acts of the defendant in this instance to have proceeded from the combination and confederacy to subvert the King's authority, the defendant was properly chargeable with them under this indictment; and that, in forming their judgment of this and all the other facts detailed in evidence, they should take into view all the circumstances of time and place, and of action, in determining the character of the several transactions. With respect to the written agreement, by which they bound themselves to resist the British laws, he thought that was sufficiently proved with regard to the American citizens; but it was not made out in proof that this was the same paper which was handed to the French settlers; but the learned Judge said that he could not admit of any distinction in this respect between aliens being under the jurisdiction and protection of the British laws and natural born subjects; the former owed a local allegiance; and what would be a breach of the laws by the one, would be so by the other,

The learned Judge, in closing, stated, that if, in determining the present case, this court was to undertake to enter upon a question of a conflict of rights between the two nations, it might be disposed to approach it with a degree of trepidation: but this case was altogether unembarrassed by any such considerations. It presented a chain of evidence of clear possession and undisturbed jurisdiction on the part of this Province from the period of its first erection down to the present time—a space of more than forty years. One of the oldest inhabitants in the Madawaska settlement had proved that he removed thither from the lower part of this Province forty years ago; that he, and all the settlers there, always considered themselves as living under this Government. It is also proved that these inhabitants have received grants of land from this Government, and have, from the beginning, been enrolled in the militia; that they have voted at elections for the county of York; have applied to the Provincial courts for redress in all suits at law; and have uniformly exercised all the privileges, and been subject to all the duties, of other inhabitants of the Province; excepting only that the sheriff states that he has not summoned them to attend on juries at Frederickton by reason of their great distance; but he expressly declared that he has always been in the habit of serving writs throughout the whole of that settlement, as much as in any other part of his bailiwick. It appears also that the defendant, Baker, considered himself as living within the territory, and under the jurisdiction of this Province; that he applied to Mr. Morehouse, the Provincial magistrate for processes to recover his debts from inhabitants in the Madawaska settlement; that he received the Provincial bounty for grain raised on land, which there can be no question is the land on which he now resides, and this on his own affidavit, stating himself to be John Baker, of the parish of Kent. It further appears that he attended a Provincial Surveyor in laying out this very land, for which a warrant of survey, under the authority of the Province, was in a course of execution, giving directions as to the course of the lines; the grant being intended for the benefit of Baker, although it was to be taken out in the name of Nevers, a British subject. Baker himself, also, had an intention of being naturalized, and stated to one of the witnesses, Mr. George West, that he had resided the necessary time, and wished to know

what other steps were necessary for this purpose. This
conversation taking place on the spot where he lived, at
the head of the Madawaska settlement, and at a time
when logs cut by him had been seized as being cut on
crown lands without license; and Baker claimed to be
dealt favorably with by reason of his residence within
the Province, and his intention to become naturalized.
The learned Judge also stated that it appeared from the
evidence that there was no line of division to be drawn
between any parts of that whole settlement, as to the
possession and exercise of jurisdiction by this Province;
that he could not imagine any principle upon which any
such line of division could be made; that one of the
witnesses spoke of the settlement having, when he first
knew it, commenced seven miles above the Great Falls;
that it has since extended downwards to within two or
three miles of the Falls. It has also been gradually
extending upwards, and all the inhabitants, in every part
of it, were equally under the jurisdiction of this Province, and entitled to the benefit and protection of its
laws; and if they were to be transferred from this jurisdiction and protection, it must be by some act of the
King's Government, competent for that purpose.

The learned Judge, with these observations, left the
case to the Jury, directing them to consider it in the
same light, and to give the defendant the benefit of the
same considerations, that they would in the case of any
other inhabitants of the Province.

The jury retired from the box, and, after about an
hour's deliberation, returned into court with a verdict of
guilty.

The defendant was then required to enter into recognizance to appear on Monday next to receive the sentence
of the court. The same bail were accepted as before, in
the same amount.

The Attorney General stated to the court that he should enter a noli prosequi on the ex-officio information which had been filed against the defendant; and also on the indictment which had been found against John Baker and six others for a riot, so far as regarded the present defendant.

The witnesses were informed that their further attendance would not be required.

Monday, May 12, 1828.

Present: His Honor the Chief Justice, Judge Bliss, and Judge Chipman.

The defendant being called, and appearing, the Attorney General proceeded to make several observations on the case, and concluded by moving the judgment of the court.

His Honor, Mr. Justice Bliss, then inquired of the defendant if he had anything to say in mitigation, or any affidavits to produce.

The defendant said he had little to say. He was brought there, and made amenable to the jurisdiction of the court, and must of course submit. He had no affidavits to produce: there were some facts, which, if they had been brought forward, might have been material; but as he was not prepared with the whole, he had thought it better not to adduce any proof. He concluded by submitting himself to the consideration of the court.

Mr. Justice Bliss then proceeded to pass sentence to the following effect:

That the defendant had been indicted by the grand jury of the county of York for a seditious conspiracy, entered into by him and others, within the jurisdiction of this court, to which he had pleaded not guilty, alleging, at the same time, that he did not consider himself amenable to the process of this court, being a citizen of the United States, and that the offence charged was committed within their territory; but the court could not admit this to be the case, it appearing clearly that the Madawaska settlement where the offence was committed, has been, from the first erection of the Province, hitherto under our laws, and subject to our jurisdiction; and that the defendant, after a very fair and full investigation of the case, had been convicted by a jury of the country; and it now remains for the court to pass their sentence upon him for this offence; in doing which their object was to treat him with that lenity which, so far as was consistent with the end of justice, is uniformly extended to His Majesty's natural born subjects; and, although the court considered the offence of which he had been found guilty of a very aggravated nature, they have had regard to his previous long imprisonment; and their object being to secure the future peace of the country, and not to pass a vindictive sentence personally against him, they had awarded the punishment accordingly; and did sentence him to be imprisoned in the common gaol of the county of York for the term of two calendar months, and to pay a fine to our lord the King of twenty five pounds, and remain committed until the same was paid.

The defendant John Baker was then taken into custody by the Sheriff.

Defence of the Frontier of Maine.

A communication in relation to this subject has been made by the Secretary of War, in compliance with a resolution, to the U. S. Senate. It contains a variety of documents, and among them the reports of Gen. Wool and Major Graham, of a reconnoissance of our

Frontier made by them the past summer. This reconnoissance was made in obedience to instructions from the
War Department, given in consequence of the repre-
sentations to the department by Gov. Kent, and the
earnest solicitations made by him of the importance of
such a movement, and the necessity of having our
frontier better fortified. We shall give such portions
of these reports as will be of interest to our readers,
commencing with Gen. Wool's.

From the Report of Brigadier General John E. Wool to
the Secretary of the Treasury.

Head Quarters, Troy, N. Y.
October 30, 1838.

Sir:

Herewith, I have the honor to transmit a report of
the military reconnoissance of the frontier of Maine,
made during the summer past, in obedience to instructions received from the War Department, dated the 12th
May and 16th of June last.

Agreeably to your verbal instructions communicated
at Washington, I repaired to Augusta, (Maine.) and
conferred with his Excellency Edward Kent, on the subject of the reconnoissance required. He not only
appeared much pleased with the object, but offered every
assistance in his power to aid in its prosecution. I
remained at Augusta until I was joined, the 28th June,
by Major Graham and Lieutenant Johnson, of the topo-
graphical engineers. On the 29th of June, we proceeded to Bangor, where I was delayed until the 3d of
July, in consequence of some preparations on the part
of Major Graham, before he could commence his topo-
graphical sketches or surveys. The Major having completed his arrangements, we set out on the 3d of July

for the examination of the northwestern frontier of the State, confining ourselves within the undisputed limits, as prescribed by your instructions of the 16th June.

After exploring Moosehead lake, Moose River, and the country west of Moosehead lake as far as the highlands which divide the State of Maine from Lower Canada, I selected a position for the establishment of a military post for the protection and defense of the northwestern frontier of the State, on the height about one mile north of Moose river, fourteen miles south of the line, on the road called the Canada road, leading to Quebec. This position is a commanding one, and would be highly important if by any circumstance England should be induced to invade Maine, from the direction of Quebec or Lower Canada. It is situated on the only route by which a military force would attempt to penetrate the country from Lower Canada. Any other route would be attended with almost insurmountable difficulties, and could not fail to retard the advance of any army. On either side of the Canada road, for nearly or quite forty miles south of the line, the country is unsettled and covered with a dense forest, through which roads must be cut and made, streams bridged, and boats built, and where neither forage, provisions or any other supplies could be obtained. If England, however, should make war upon the United States in order to secure the possession of the disputed territory in question, she would not waste her resources by contending for it in the wilds or dense forests of Maine. Having an army and a navy at her disposal, she would endeavor to compel the U. States to a cession of it by the destruction of our commerce, navy depots, commercial cities and frontier towns. These, with the present disposition of the military establishment of the country constitute our vulnerable points, and of which England would not fail to take advantage. She would neither send her armies into our forests, nor into the heart of the country, from whence it is not probable they would return. She may, however, threaten Maine, from Quebec, and perhaps carry on a predatory warfare, by means of the Canada road. To protect the frontier and prevent such inroads upon the people, I would establish a post with two companies of infantry, near Moose river, with a post of observation on the height of land dividing Maine from Lower Canada. The depot of supplies for those posts I would establish on the south side of Moose river, one mile from the principal post. The Kennebec forks I would designate as a principal depot and place of concentration for the militia of that section of the country.

The heights surrounding the forks are well calculated for defence, and would enable a small force, well directed, to hold a larger one in check until the militia of the country could be collected.

Before closing this part of my report it may not be improper to remark, that a road has been cut out, but not made, north of the military position selected near Moose river, leading from the Canada road to the head of Moosehead Lake. It has been suggested that a military force from Quebec or Lower Canada, might penetrate Maine by that road and Moosehead lake. In answer to which I have only to observe that no general, who understood his profession, would invade Maine by any route destitute of forage, provisions, or the means of transportation. On the contrary, he would take the route that would furnish the greatest amount of supplies, and the greatest facilities of marching into the heart of the country. To take the route referred to, he would be compelled to make roads, construct bridges and boats, and to carry with him his forage, provisions, and the means of land transportation. In such a case, it would require no foresight to predict the result. He would beyond all question be defeated, if the people of Maine were true to themselves, and true to the country.

Deeming no other posts than those above mentioned necessary for the defence or protection of the north-western frontier of Maine, I returned to Bangor, leaving Major Graham and Lieutenant Johnson to make the required surveys and sketches.

On the 16th of July, accompanied by his Excellency Edward Kent, I set out to examine the eastern and northeastern frontier of the State.—On the 17th, we examined the military position at Houlton, which I con-sider well calculated for the defence and protection of that region of country. With proper works, and a gar-rison composed of six companies of infantry, and two of artillery, I do not believe any attempt would be made from New Brunswick to invade the disputed territory, or by that route to invade the settled parts of Maine. A general commanding at Fredericton, or St. Johns, with a large disposable force, might attempt an enterprise against the garrison at Houlton, intercept its communi-cation with, and cut off its retreat to Bangor.—This might be done by way of Woodstock, Eel river, or the Lakes Magaguadaweek and Chiputnaticook, or Grand Lake. From Woodstock, through by roads, the Mili-tary road could be reached five miles south and in the rear of Houlton. By Eel river and Dunn's on the Calais road, the same point could be reached. By the lakes above mentioned, and Butterfield's on the Calais road, the military road could be intercepted by a cross road, eight miles south of the Mattawamkeag forks, and about thirty eight miles south of Houlton.

This route will be the shortest from Fredericton and in the winter the easiest to be accomplished. It is, however, not probable that in the present wild state of the country, no roads being made except from Fredericton to Woodstock, any movement of the kind would be made with eight companies of regular troops at Houlton and a respectable force at Calais. Such a movement by the British forces would undoubtedly produce a corresponding one on the part of the United States troops at Calais, against Fredericton or St. Johns, which, unless the British were in great force at those places, would produce a recall of any movement against Houlton or the disputed territory. No military commander would hazard an enterprise against Houlton or the disputed territory, if by such a movement he could possibly lose Fredericton or St. Johns which would give to the conquerors the finest part of New Brunswick.

To guard against any movement as suggested, I would recommend that a regiment of infantry and two companies of artillery be stationed at Calais, and one company of infantry and one of artillery at Eastport, with posts of observation at Butterfield's and Dunn's on the Calais road, leading to Houlton. From Calais, Fredericton or St. Johns might be reached in three days. Should the above recommendations be adopted, I would designate Calais as a proper place for the main depot of supplies and concentration of the militia for the defence of the eastern frontier; and the Mattawamkeag forks for the depot and concentration of the militia for the defence of the disputed territory and the northeastern frontier.

In addition to the above, I would recommend the erection of an arsenal near Bangor, on the right or left bank of the Penobscot. Also a fortification and garrison at the entrance of both the Penobscot and Kennebec.

From a statement received from his excellency Edward Kent, it would appear that the militia of Maine exceeds forty-one thousand.

Of these, in the course of ten days, 4,500 could be collected at the forks of the Kennebec, 4,000 at the Mattawamkeag forks, and 2,500 at Calais. In twenty days there could be 12,000 collected at the Kennebec forks, 10,000 at the Mattawamkeag forks and 8,000 at Calais.

The above calculation, however, is made up on the supposition that they would be called out as organized by regiments and brigades. A draft would take a longer period, but the same number of men could be obtained.

It would also appear, from the same statement, that the State has in depot 9,000 muskets, 2,200 rifles, 350 pistols, and 850 swords, and a good supply of equipments, all in good order and fit for service. The arms and equipments, however, in the possession of the militia, are generally small, and too light for active service.

I am, very respectfully, your obedient survent,
JOHN E. WOOL.

To the Hon. J. R. Poinsett,
Secretary of War.

Fredericton, Feb. 13, 1839.

By His Excellency Major General Sir John Harvey, K. C. B. and K. C. H., Lieut. Governor and Commander in Chief of the Province of New Brunswick, etc. etc. etc.

John Harvey.

A Proclamation.

Whereas, I have received information that a party of armed persons to the number of two hundred or more, have invaded a portion of this province, under the jurisdiction of Her Majesty's Government, from the neighbor-

ing State of Maine, for the professed object of exercising authority, and driving off persons stated to be cutting therein—and that divers other persons have without any legal authority, taken up arms for the purpose of resisting such invasion and outrage, and have broken open certain stores in Woodstock, in which Arms and Ammunition belonging to Her Majesty were deposited, and have taken the same away for that purpose—I do hereby charge and command all persons concerned in such illegal acts, forthwith to return the Arms and Ammunition, so illegally taken, to their place of deposite, as the Government of the Province will take care to adopt all necessary measures for resisting any hostile invasion or outrage that may be attempted upon any part of Her Majesty's Territory or Subjects.

And I do hereby charge and command all Magistrates, Sheriffs, and other officers, to be vigilant, aiding and assisting in the apprehension of all persons so offending, and to bring them to justice, And in order to aid and assist the Civil Power in that respect, if necessary, I have ordered sufficient Military Force to proceed forthwith to the places where these Outrages are represented to have been committed as well to prevent Foreign invasion, as to prevent the illegal assumption of Arms by her Majesty's Subjects in this Province.

And further, in order to be prepared, if necessary to call in the aid of the Constitutional Militia Force of the country. I do hereby charge and command the officers commanding the first and second Battalions of the militia of the County of Carleton, forthwith to proceed as the Law directs, to the drafting of a body of men, to consist of one fourth of the strength of each of these battalions, to be in readiness for actual service, should occasion require.

Given under my Hand and Seal at Fredericton, the
Thirteenth day of February, in the year of our
Lord one thousand eight hundred and thirty-
nine, and in the second year of Her Majesty's
reign.

By his Excellency's Command.

WM. F. ODELL.

(Whig Editorial, Feb. 6, 1839.)

THE AROOSTOOK EXPEDITION.

When we first heard of the capture of the Land Agent
and several others, and the sudden retreat of the Sheriff
with his posse, we supposed in common with most of
our fellow citizens here, that this was effected by a small
body of trespassers, who would hold together only a few
days, and that the prisoners would be released after a
short detention—and that this whole matter in the way
it had been conducted and terminated, was a fair subject of ridicule, and was treated accordingly. It was a
proper subject of game, which any one had a right to
hunt down. We wish, however, to be understood, that
we are wholly in favor of the object of this expedition,
we feel desirous of seeing our country protected and
jurisdiction enforced within our territorial lines according
to the treaty of 1783.

If the Provincial Government have interferred in this
matter by arresting and imprisoning any of our citizens,
in the rightful exercise of their legal duties within our
own territory, we stand ready to shoulder our musket
and take our chance in the front rank of our militia—
and entertain not the slightest doubt but that the whole
body of our citizens would rise as one man, to defend
the territory purchased by the blood of our fathers.

But we have the right to demand that wise counsellors and energetic men shall move in this business and stand at the head of affairs—not such brawling and noisy politicians, such weak, inefficient and feather-bed men as have recently been shoved forward into this Aroostook expedition and have disgraced it. We have no desire to throw the slightest obstacle in the way of this affair, and it gives us great pleasure to learn that Jonathan P. Rogers, Esq. has been despatched by the Governor and Council, to hold an interview with Sir John Harvey, in reference to this business.

If Gov. Fairfield had taken this step in the first place, as Gov. Kent did in reference to the Boundary Commissioners, there would have been little or no trouble in driving off the trespassers from the disputed territory. But this, the Governor was unwilling to do, after his party had reviled and ridiculed Gov. Kent, in the manner they have done, for the course he took. Having now begun this business upon the Whig policy pursued by Gov. Kent, we cannot doubt of a successful issue.

(Editorial in Whig, Feb. 22, 1839.)

STEADY.

Our State has been for the 3d time invaded and our citizens forcibly arrested, carried away and incarcerated in a FOREIGN JAIL. The first time, Mr. Baker and his neighbors, next Mr. Greely, and now the Land Agent and his assistants. We have remonstrated and entreated long enough and to no purpose. We now appeal to arms. We now appeal to the law of nature, recognized by all communities, for that protection which has been denied us by the General Government. Be the issue what it may, upon this question the whole State is united to a man, and will carry into the conflict its undivided energies. As we are in this city in the midst of a great excitement it behooves us all to keep calm and cool and proceed with the utmost deliberation. Expresses are passing every day through this city from the Aroostook and from the Province to Augusta and back——our streets for the last two days have been filled with the busy preparations for the Aroostook expedition. The artillery has been forwarded and large quantities of amunition, provisions, forage, etc. Twenty men are engaged at the Foundry casting balls. Bodies of volunteers from the country are passing through the city hourly, and not less than 500 are now between this place and Matawamkeag Point. The draft of one thousand men has been made in this division, and they will all be on the march to morrow.

(Whig Correspondence.)

Friday, 9 o'clock. A. M.

Aroostook Expedition.

The remainder of the detachment have left the city, and somewhat of the intense excitement is abated which has pervaded our own citizens, and the crowd of spectators which have thronged the city. Most of the detachment left the city yesterday in small squads, and this arrangement of the march we hope will secure comfortable and warm quarters to the zealous and patriotic Militia. Every aid will be given by the citizens along the line to the proper officers, and the men will be received in the most kind and hospitable manner. The appearance of the troops was such as excited our surprise and admiration. Coming together at a moments notice, every man seemed to be prepared for duty and eager to reach the scene of operations. The Commander in Chief ordered, we understand, a rendezvous of the force on Thursday at 10 o'clock, most of which, we have said, left town the same day, and the remainder this morning. The promptitude with which the call of the Commanding General has been obeyed and the order and enthusiasm of the troops and the universal impression of the ability and energy of the Commanding General, has impressed the whole community with a full confidence in its success.

(Editorial in Whig, Feb. 23, 1839.)

THE ASSERTION OF THE AGE.

The assertion of the Age, that we wished to cast ridicule on the Aroostook Expedition, is wholly false. We shall not bandy words with a paper which thus attempts to turn the present crisis to political account. We did think it strange that the person entrusted with the command, should have suffered himself to have been taken in the manner he was. We are not opposed to the Expedition, and never have been, and as long as it is conducted properly we shall not utter a syllable against it. The Whigs of the State have but one wish, one opinion, in regard to the course to be pursued—they are anxious that Gov. Fairfield should go on, without faltering in the least;—we hope that he will not, and that the State will not retrace a single step, in the position she has taken. A holier spirit than that of party, should now animate the people. The crisis demands the united energy and action of all parties, and we doubt not, that the one sentiment, the one feeling, the deep enthusiasm which pervades every bosom, will continue thus universal, until the rights of our noble State are established beyond a doubt and fully and honorably recognized. The honor and interest of the whole State must be maintained at all hazards. We shall have no fears of the issue of the conflict, knowing as we do, that the citizens of Maine will not prove recreant to duty, and the obligations now resting upon them.

While we would not have the Whigs, as a party forget for a moment, the ancient landmarks, of their political faith, and the strong grounds of their opposition to the State and National Administrations,—so neither would we have them, in the least, abate in their ardor and anxiety to bring our boundary rights to a successful termination. Though we may have occasion, hereafter, to revert to the conduct and management of certain individuals at the commencement of this interesting enterprise, we shall not be backward in upholding the great object which the State, as one people, has in view. The present movement we should regard as National, and we shall not be found wanting in the bold maintenance of the honor and welfare of the State.

(Whig Correspondence.)

FROM HOULTON.

Tuesday, 9 o'clock A. M.

An express has just arrived from the Aroostook bringing the information that our Land Agent has been put into close jail. Just look at the contrast. The British Land Agent was brought here in a coach with four horses, a prisoner, carried to the Bangor House, and invited to one of the best rooms in the House, and received the best of fare, while our Agent was dragged on a horse sled to Frederickton and incarcerated within the walls of a prison. Should not such treatment cause the blood of every American to boil with indignation?

11 o'clock A. M.

The Augusta Light Infantry Company has just arrived in this city.

(Whig Correspondence.)

Saturday, 5 o'clock, P. M.

A company of Cavalry, consisting of 48 men, have just arrived in this city from Waldo county.

We have just seen a gentleman who left the Aroostook on Thursday. The volunteers have erected a fort with logs, and have five field pieces mounted. They were all in fine spirits. The Waldo volunteers, the Piscataquis volunteers, and the Brewer volunteers, arrived at No. 4, about 36 miles this side of the camp on Thursday night. The Bangor Artillery and Dexter Artillery arrived at Lincoln on Friday night, and the Dexter Rifle corps were about 5 miles this side of Lincoln on Saturday morning.

Four of the British Regular troops, deserters from the Provinces, arrived at Lincoln on Friday night. Desertions are taking place daily, and some of these liberty-loving fellows have already enlisted in one of the companies of the 3d Division. The "stars and stripes" will coax many of her Majesty's subjects to their ample folds.

GOVERNOR FAIRFIELD'S ADDRESS TO TROOPS.

Fellow Soldiers:—An unfounded, unjust, and insulting claim of title has been made by the British Government to more than one-third of the whole territory of your State. More than this, it insists upon having exclusive jurisdiction and possession until its claims of title is settled——while in the meantime its subjects are stripping this territory of its valuable growth of timber, in defiance of your authority and your power. A few days since you sent a civil force under your Land Agent, to drive off these bands of armed plunderers and protect your property from their work of devastation. But the Agent while employed in the performance of this duty,

with two of his assistants, were seized, transported
beyond the bounds of the State, and incarcerated in a
foreign jail under British authorities.   Those who remain
are threatened with a forcible expulsion by British
troops, if they do not immediately leave the territory
and abandon your property to proffered protection of
Her Majesty's Lieutenant Governor.   And perhaps
before this moment, your soil has not only been polluted
by the invader's footsteps, but the blood of our citizens
may have been shed by British Myrmidons.

The Age states that part of the detachment left for
the frontier on Wednesday, and the remainder on Thursday morning.

(From Maine Newspapers, 1839.)

THE SOLDIERS SONG.

Tune—Auld Lang Syne.

We are marching on to Madawask,
To fight the trespassers;
We'll teach the British how to walk—
And come off conquerors.

We'll have our land right good and clear,
For all the English say;
They shall not cut another log,
Nor stay another day.

They need not think to have our land,
We Yankees can fight well;
We've whipped them twice most manfully,
As every child can tell.

And if the Tyrants say one word,
A third time we will show,
How high the Yankee spirit runs,
And what our guns can do.

They better much all stay at home,
And mind their business there;
The way we treated them before,
Made all the Nations stare.

Come on! brace fellows, one and all!
The Red-coats ne'er shall say,
We Yankees, feared to meet them armed,
So gave our land away.

We'll feed them well with ball and shot.
We'll cut these Red-coats down,
Before we yield to them an inch
Or title of our ground.

Ye Husbands, Fathers, Brothers, Sons,
From every quarter come!
March, to the bugle and the fife!
March, to the beating drum!

Onward! my Lads so brave and true
Our Country's right demands
With justice, and with glory fight,
For these Aroostook lands.

Bangor, Feb. 21, 1839.

(From Maine Newspapers, 1839.)

MAINE BATTLE SONG.

Come, sogers! take your muskets up,
    And grasp your faithful rifles:
We're going to lick the red coat men,
    Who call us yankees, "trifles."
Bring out the big gun made of brass,
    Which forges July thunder;
Bring out the flag of Bennington,
    And strike the foe with wonder.

We'll lick the red coats any how,
    And drive them from our border:
The loggers are awake—and all
    Await the Gin'rals order;
Britannia shall not rule the Maine,
    Nor shall she rule the water;
They've sung that song full long enough,
    Much longer than they oughter.

The Aroostook's right slick stream,
    Has nation sights of woodlands,
And hang the feller that would lose
    His footing on such good lands.

And all along the boundary line
    There's pasturing for cattle;
But where that line of boundary is,
    We must decide by battle.

We do not care about the land,
    But they shan't hook it from us;
Our country, right or wrong, we cry—
    No budging or compromise.
So—beat the sheepskin blow the fife,
    And march in training order;
Our wave is through the wilderness,
    And all along the border.

Head Quarters, Eastern Division, ⎫
        United States, Army, ⎬
Augusta, Me. March 21, 1839. ⎭

The undersigned, a Major General in the Army of
the United States being specially charged with maintaining the peace and safety of their entire Northern and
Eastern Frontiers, having cause to apprehend a collision
of arms between the proximate forces of New Brunswick
and the State of Maine on the disputed territory which
is claimed by both, has the honor, in the sincere desire
of the United States to preserve the relations of peace
and amity with Great Britain—relations which might be
much endangered by such untoward collison—to invite
from His Excellency Major General Sir John Harvey,
Lieutenant Governor, etc. etc.,—a general declaration
to this effect.

That it is not the intention of the Lieutenant Governor of Her Brittannic Majesty's Province of New
Brunswick, under the expected renewal of negociations
between the Cabinets of London and Washington on the
subject of the said disputed territory, without renewed
instructions to that effect from his Government, to seek
to take the Military possession of that territory, or to

seek to expel therefrom the armed Civil posse, or the troops of Maine.

Should the undersigned have the honor to be favored with such declaration or assurance to be by him communicated to his Excellency the Governor of the State of Maine, the undersigned does not in the least doubt that he would be immediately and fully authorized by the Governor of Maine to communicate to his Excellency, the Lieutenant Governor of New Brunswick a corresponding pacific declaration to this effect:—

That in the hope of a speedy and satisfactory settlement, by negociation between the Governments of the United States and Great Britain of the principal or boundary question between the State of Maine and the Province of New Brunswick, it is not the intention of the Governor of Maine, without renewed instructions from the Legislature of the State, to attempt to disturb by arms, the said Province in the possession of the Madawaska settlements, or to attempt to interrupt the usual communications between that Province and Her Majesty's Upper Provinces; and that he is willing in the mean time, to leave the question of possession and jurisdiction as they at present stand; that is, Great Britain, holding, in fact, possession of a part of the said territory and the Government of Maine denying her right to such possession; and the State of Maine holding, in fact, possession of another portion of the same territory to which her right is denied by Great Britain.

With this understanding the Governor of Maine will, without unnecessary delay, withdraw the Military force of the State from the said disputed territory—leaving only, under a Land Agent, a small civil posse, armed or unarmed, to protect the timber recently cut, and to prevent future depredations.

Reciprocal assurance of the foregoing friendly character having been, through the undersigned, interchanged, all danger of collision between the immediate parties to the controversy will be at once removed, and time allowed the United States and Great Britain to settle amicably the great question of limits.

The undersigned has much pleasure in renewing to His Excellency, Major General Sir John Harvey the assurances of his ancient high consideration and respect.

WINFIELD SCOTT.

To a copy of the foregoing, Sir John Harvey annexed the following:—

The undersigned, Major General Sir John Harvey, Lieutenant Governor of Her Britannic Majesty's Province of New Brunswick, having received a proposition from Major General Winfield Scott of the United States Army, of which the foregoing is a copy, hereby, on his part, signifies his concurrence and acquiescence therein.

Sir John Harvey renews with great pleasure to Major General Scott, the assurance of his warmest personal consideration, regard and respect.

J. HARVEY.

Government House, Fredericton,
New Brunswick, March 23, 1839.

To a paper containing the note of General Scott, and the acceptance of Sir John Harvey, Governor Fairfield annexed his acceptance in these words:

Executive Department, ⎱
Augusta, March 25, 1839. ⎰

The undersigned, Governor of Maine, in consideration of the foregoing, the exigency for calling out the troops of Maine have ceased, has no hesitation in signifying his entire acquiescence in the proposition of Major General Scott.

The undersigned has the honor to tender to Major General Scott the assurance of his high respect and esteem.

JOHN FAIRFIELD.

(From Bangor Whig, April 12, 1839.)

THE SOLDIER'S RETURN.

On Wednesday evening, about 6 o'clock, the Bangor Independent Volunteers marched into the city, under command of Lieut. Dunning, on their return from the Aroostook. The Company numbered about fifty, principally young men, who are known as among the most respectable and enterprising of the city. We were rejoiced to preceive so much interest and spirit manifested at their return. They marched with a firm and elastic step, to the tune of Home! Sweet Home! The appropriateness of the music to the ocassion, excited one common impulse of satisfaction. We have rarely known an instance which appealed so directly to the heart.

Tuesday evening, the Hancock Guards, a rifle company, under command of Capt. Wing, arrived, also. This is a fine company, from Castine and Bluehill. They were furnished for the campaign with Hall's Patent Rifles.

The appearance and bearing of these Companies do honor to the Militia of the State, and to their commander, Gen. Hodsdon. They have discipline and skill, almost equal to regular troops and perform the duties of the soldier in a manner deserving great praise. Let those who have been induced to speak lightly of the militia system, view these men and ask themselves, where else they would look for defence of our country against foreign aggression. And who are the men who deserve sympathy and respect, if not those who so willingly have borne the hardships and privations of a winter campaign exposed to all the fatigues they are called upon to endure.

Gen. Hodsdon, a few days ago, ordered Col. Stevens to Bangor, to cause temporary Barracks to be erected on Thomas's Hill for the accommodation of the troops on their return. They will rendezvous at this place and be paid off as fast as may be convenient. It will however, be a work of several days. The men were principally supplied with arms by the State, and their old guns will be returned to them when the State's arms are surrended. As the troops will come in by companies or small detachments, some days must necessarily elapse, before they can be paid off and disbanded.

We think Gen. Hodsdon deserves much praise for his forethought in this matter. We all recollect the inconvenience of quartering 600 men under Gen. Bachelder's command in the midst of the city. Besides, these soldiers deserve better treatment, after their long march through the mud, than to be crowded in large companies of 50 or 60 men, into a room or two, 15 by 18, at this season of the year. We suppose they will be reviewed here by Gen. Hodsdon, and our citizens gratified by a display of their military discipline.

LETTER FROM JAMES SULLIVAN.

Scoodiac Falls, Sept'r 29th, 1796.

Brother:

I came here with a hope to see you—I am agent for the United States to appear before men who are appointed to find the river the United States and the King called St. Croix when the States became a great nation. The men who are come and coming, want to hear what your old men can tell them truly on that question. I invite you to come before them with three or four of your old men at St. Andrews on friday the next week. I want you to tell them what is there and I will pay you for your time what ever is right——

Brother:

You know that the United States is your friend——you know that Massachusetts considers your tribe as her children and you will not be unwilling to come at their call to tell the truth.

I am your Brother
JAMES SULLIVAN.

To Francis Joseph Governor the
Passimaquody Indians.

CPSIA information can be obtained at www.ICGtesting.com

232060LV00007B/51/A

9 780548 677575